# THE USBORNE ENCYCLOPEDIA OF
# WORLD RELIGIONS

## Susan Meredith and Clare Hickman

### Edited by Kirsteen Robson

### Designed by Karen Tomlins, Nicky Wainwright, Leonard Le Rolland, Adam Constantine and Joanne Kirkby

### Consultant: Dr Wendy Dossett

Additional consultants: The Baptist Union of Great Britain; Bharatiya Vidya Bhavan (Institute of Indian Art and Culture); The Board of Deputies of British Jews; British Humanist Association; The British Taoist Association; The Church of Scotland; Professor Peter Clarke; *The Congregationalist*; The First Church of Christ, Scientist; Professor Gavin Flood; The General Assembly of Unitarian and Free Christian Churches; The General Conference of Seventh-day Adventists; Stephen Hodge; International Shinto Foundation; Dr Will Johnson; London Mennonite Centre; The Methodist Church of Great Britain; Dr Anne Millard; The Muslim Educational Trust; Nazarene Theological College, Manchester; Quaker Association Headquarters; Rabbi Danny Rich; Salvation Army UK Headquarters; Indarjit Singh OBE, JP; Jan Thompson (RE Adviser); UK National Baha'i Centre; UK Public Affairs Department of The Church of Jesus Christ of Latter-day Saints; United Pentecostal Church International; United Reformed Church; Dr Maya Warrier; Watch Tower Bible and Tract Society of Britain; World Bible School; The World Zoroastrian Organisation; Pastor Eva Wunderlich; Dr Xinzhong Yao

# THE USBORNE ENCYCLOPEDIA OF
# WORLD
# RELIGIONS

## Usborne Quicklinks

At the Usborne Quicklinks website, you will find links to over 250 websites chosen to enhance the information in this book. To visit the sites, go to **www.usborne-quicklinks.com** and type the keywords "world religions".

Here are some of the things you can do at the websites we recommend:

- Take virtual tours of places of worship
- Watch video clips of stories, myths and teachings from different religions
- Listen to all kinds of religious music
- Discover paintings and architecture inspired by faith
- Browse photo galleries of religious festivals and artifacts

## Internet safety

When using the internet, make sure you follow the internet safety guidelines displayed at the Usborne Quicklinks website.

## Websites about different religions

The recommended websites have been selected by Usborne editors to enrich the information in this book and are not intended to promote any particular beliefs or viewpoints. The views expressed at the websites are held by people of different religious backgrounds and give an interesting insight into the diversity of world religions. Please note Usborne Publishing is not responsible for the content or availability of any website other than its own.

For information about how to use the internet safely, go to the Help and advice area at the Usborne Quicklinks website.

## Dates and abbreviations

You are probably used to seeing the abbreviations BC and AD next to dates. BC stands for Before Christ and AD stands for Anno Domini (in the Year of the Lord). Both terms refer to the birth of Jesus Christ.

This book uses the abbreviation BCE instead of BC, and CE instead of AD. BCE and CE stand for Before the Common Era and Common Era. These terms are acceptable to all religions. Where you see a date without BCE or CE after it, you can assume that it is CE.

Historians are uncertain of some exact dates in early religious history, so these dates begin with the abbreviation "c". This stands for "circa", which is Latin for "about". The period known as the Middle Ages is generally taken to be from about 1000 to 1500CE.

## Numbers of followers

The numbers of followers of religions as stated in this book are approximate, and you may find other books or websites quoting different membership numbers. There are several reasons for this.

Some people refuse to enter their religion on official forms. Others may enter the religion of their country or parents, although they don't actually follow it themselves. In some places, such as China or Japan, many people follow more than one religion. Religions often compete for members, and religious officials may overestimate the number of members of their own faith.

# CONTENTS

# WHAT IS RELIGION?

Throughout history and across the world, people have asked questions about where the world came from, who they are, and what their purpose is in life. These questions have different answers for different people. Some say that there is more to life than just the physical world, and some say that by living life in a certain way the answers can be found. Many people call these answers "the Truth", or Absolute or Ultimate reality.

Many people believe that prayer will bring them closer to an ultimate power which exists beyond the everyday world. This girl is praying at a temple ceremony in Bali, Indonesia.

## A spiritual dimension

The ultimate reality is known as a spiritual, not a physical, one. It is difficult to talk about because, unlike most scientific facts, it lies beyond what can be known in the usual way.

Religious people would say that although the spirit cannot really be described, its presence can be felt. It is what gives something its innermost essence and distinctive character. In ancient times, the spirit was often described as the spark or breath which gave life. Anything which helps people get closer to the spiritual world is said to be sacred or holy and is treated with respect.

Carvings like this on poles are sacred to Native North Americans. They represent guardian animals, known as totems.

## Explaining religion

The word for religion comes from the Latin *religio*, which means "a duty". Many religions expect their believers to behave according to a set of guidelines or rules. In some languages, for example, the Indian languages, there was no such word as religion for a long time. Religion was so much a part of everyday life that a special word was not needed for it.

Today, it is hard to explain the word religion in a way which everyone finds acceptable. Nevertheless, there are some ideas which many religions have in common.

## A supreme power

Religion usually, though not always, involves showing respect or offering worship to a higher unseen power which is thought to have created the world and now oversees it. This higher power is sometimes known as the Absolute. In some religions the Absolute is seen as God, or is represented by many gods or goddesses, who are also known as deities. God, or the deities, are asked for help and guidance. Some religions, such as Buddhism, do not believe in a creator god, and instead teach about overcoming suffering.

Most religions teach that the supreme power is beyond description and so they do not have pictures of it. Jews do not even say the name of their God aloud because it is so holy, and they write it in the shortened form, YHWH.

High places are often significant in religion. It is as though these places reach beyond the physical world toward the spiritual. This statue of Jesus Christ is on top of Corcovado Mountain in Brazil.

## The soul

In many religions there is a belief that people, and in some cases animals, have a kind of inner spark, which is separate from their body and mind, and which corresponds to the spirit. It is often called the spirit or soul. It is considered the most important part of a person's being because it is what can lead toward the Absolute. In many religions, the soul is believed to be immortal. This means that it never dies.

## The big questions

Religions ask and try to answer certain important questions. Why was the world created? How should people live? Why is there so much suffering? What happens after a person dies? Any answers to such questions can't be tested by reason and proved; a person has to trust or have faith in them. Another word for religion is faith.

Religions recognize that the world and the people in it aren't perfect and that they cause suffering. According to many religions, if people have faith and follow the religion's teachings correctly, then their lives will be transformed. These people will ultimately be united with the Absolute and be freed from suffering. This is often called salvation or liberation.

┌─INTERNET LINKS─┐
For links to websites where you can find out more about what religion is and find different ideas about the creation of the universe, go to **www.usborne-quicklinks.com**

7

## Worship

Worship involves showing respect and devotion to a deity. Believers often gather together to express the feelings of wonder, joy and thanks that they share. When the meeting takes the form of a ceremony it is often called a service. Set actions that are performed in worship are called rituals. It is through them that people show their beliefs.

Muslims wash themselves before worship, as a sign of respect to God.

Common rituals of worship are to cover the head as a sign of modesty and equality with other people, and to kneel or bow down to show respect for the deity. In some religions, often those that began in hot, dusty countries, people also wash and take off their shoes before worship.

## Prayer and meditation

Prayer often consists of giving praise and thanks, or asking for help and guidance for oneself or other people. Through prayer, a person can build a special relationship with a deity. Prayer can also take the form of meditation. The purpose of meditation is to achieve inner stillness so that barriers to understanding fall away.

People of different religions pray in different ways. For example, some prayers are said aloud, while others are whispered or silent. In some religions, people show respect to the deity by kneeling or bowing down; in other religions it is thought respectful to pray standing up. Some people pray with their eyes shut and hands clasped or cupped together. People of many religions often use objects such as beads, candles or incense, to help them concentrate while they are praying or meditating.

In many religions people gather together for prayer and worship. The picture below shows a crowd of Muslim women praying together in Cirebon, Java.

## Scriptures

Religious writings are known as scriptures and are treated with great respect by believers. This is especially so when the scriptures are thought to have been communicated directly by God. Such direct communications are known as revelations.

The holy book of Islam, the *Qur'an*, is said to have been revealed by God. Muslims treat it with great respect, and often place it on a stand, like the one above, to read it.

Some people believe that every word of a certain scripture comes directly from God and so has unchanging authority for all time. They are known as conservatives, traditionalists or fundamentalists.

Other people may believe that the same scripture was inspired by God but feel that the social conditions of the time when it was written and the individual views and personality of the authors have to be taken into account when trying to understand it. These people are often called liberals or modernists.

## Sacred objects

In many religions, worship may take place in a particular place, such as a simple shrine in a room at home, or a huge, richly decorated temple. Worship may also involve using particular objects. These places and objects are usually considered sacred and are treated with great respect.

In some religions, such as Hinduism, people feel that only the best is good enough for the deity. They also want people to be inspired in their worship by the beauty of their surroundings and the ceremonial objects. For these reasons, buildings and objects are often crafted by highly skilled people, using the most precious materials available. Many other people feel that lavish decorations may distract people's attention from the deity. For example, in Islam, the insides of many mosques are kept plain, for this reason.

The architectural design and ornate decoration of St. Basil's Cathedral in Moscow was intended to inspire Christians to worship God.

The Chinese new year falls near the end of winter and welcomes in the spring. Noisy processions and dancing are intended to frighten off evil spirits. These men are taking part in a procession, carrying a model of a dragon to symbolize the bringing of good luck in the coming year.

## Festivals

Religious festivals often celebrate special events in the history of a religion, such as the birth or death of a leader. They also celebrate important events in nature, such as spring or harvest time. Festivals remind believers of their faith at certain times during each year and bring them together to give thanks for the things they consider to be valuable.

## Priests

Many religions have priests. These are officials who have public duties such as leading acts of worship. They may also try to guide people toward the spiritual world and in some religions act as a kind of go-between, between people and the deity, and vice versa.

There are often strict guidelines about who can become a priest. For example, in Hinduism, only men born into a particular social class can be priests. Christians disagree as to whether women should be priests. Traditionalists argue that the scriptures imply that priests should be male. The liberals say that there is no evidence for this.

┌INTERNET LINKS┐

For links to websites where you can read more about what religion is and explore features of religion such as prayer and festivals, go to **www.usborne-quicklinks.com**

9

## Sacred places

Some places are thought to have a spiritual quality. This is often because important religious events took place there. In many religions, believers may try to visit these sacred places at least once in their lifetime. Jerusalem, in Israel, for example, is sacred to Jews, Christians and Muslims alike, but for different historical reasons.

A journey to a sacred place is called a pilgrimage. If the journey is difficult, it may be thought to strengthen a person's faith all the more.

## Rites of passage

Religions usually have special ceremonies to celebrate key stages in people's lives. These events include birth, the beginning of adulthood, marriage and death. The celebrations that mark them are sometimes known as rites of passage. They encourage people to think about the meaning and purpose of life, and to help individuals through times of change. There is also the hope that those taking part will be blessed by the supreme power.

The city of Jerusalem in Israel is important to Muslims and Jews. The domed building below is a Muslim shrine called the Dome of the Rock. The wall below it, known as the Western Wall, is all that remains of an ancient Jewish temple. Both are major pilgrimage sites.

## Monks and nuns

In many religions there are groups of people who have different, stricter rules governing the way they live. The men are called monks. They live in monasteries, separated from the rest of society. The women, called nuns, live in nunneries.

Many Christian nuns wear plain, simple clothes and cover their hair. This helps them think less about their appearance and enables them to concentrate on God.

Buddhist monks and nuns wear saffron robes and carry a begging bowl. Local people give food to them. The act of giving is important in Buddhism.

Monks of the Jain religion in India believe in non-violence. This monk is sweeping the ground to avoid stepping on living creatures and he is wearing a mask to avoid breathing them in.

Monks and nuns try to lead simple, modest lives. They don't marry and most don't have ordinary jobs. Often they aren't allowed to touch money. Some spend their lives praying, meditating and studying the scriptures; others do charity work. Monks and nuns usually wear simple, plain clothes. This helps them avoid being vain, and encourages them to think of everyone as equal.

## Functions of religion

Religious people feel that what they believe in is true. People who study religions say that, true or not, religions have many functions in society.

Some experts say that in the past, religion was relied upon to explain many things that people didn't understand, such as the weather or the seasons. Now there are scientific explanations for many of these things. Many people feel that science and religion can exist alongside each other.

The Ancient Greeks believed that lightning was caused by the anger of the god Zeus.

People who study how early humans lived in social groups see religion as a force which held communities together. It gave their members shared rules for living and a shared way of understanding the world.

Psychologists look at the way religion reduces people's fears by giving them something beyond themselves to rely on. Some think this is a healthy way of coping with a difficult world. Others think that it stops people from becoming confident in what they can do for themselves.

## Other viewpoints

Not everyone in the world has a religious faith. Most people who don't have a religious faith feel that it is perfectly possible to lead a good and fulfilling life without religion.

People who don't believe that a supernatural power exists are called atheists. Others, who are called agnostics, say that it is impossible to know whether or not God exists, because there is no proof either way. As this is the case, they do not think that it is worth building their lives on unproven ideas.

Many people are humanists. They say that human beings have the capacity within themselves to develop and flourish, and to build a world which will be happier, more just and caring.

Humanists believe that this is the only life we have. They say that people should try to live full and happy lives and, by their actions, make it easier for other people to do the same. Humanists believe that all situations and people deserve to be judged on their individual merits, rather than by a rigid set of religious rules.

The picture above shows a model of a strand of DNA, the substance which controls how all living things grow and develop. Since the discovery of DNA in the mid twentieth century, much more is known about how living things reproduce. This does not stop people from feeling that the creation of new life is miraculous.

## Future of religion

Some people feel that, within the richer, developed countries of the world, religion has lost some of its importance. They believe that some people in these societies are becoming more and more obsessed with making money, and gaining material possessions, and that they have abandoned many of their religious ideals.

Over the world as a whole, though, religions are growing. In addition, some experts predict that there will be a swing away from this materialistic outlook and that people will turn back to the more spiritual values of religion.

┌─ INTERNET LINKS ─────────

For links to websites where you can read more about what religion is and examine the idea of sacredness and the beliefs of humanists, go to **www.usborne-quicklinks.com**

# HINDUISM

ॐ Hinduism is one of the world's oldest living religions, dating back to at least 2000BCE. Hinduism developed, and still flourishes, mainly in India and Nepal. Hindus do not call their religion "Hinduism", but refer to it simply as *sanatana dharma*. This means "eternal teaching" or "eternal law". There are over one billion Hindus in the world today.

The Hindu woman pictured here is bathing and praying in the River Ganges, in India. She has filled her pot with river water, which Hindus believe to be holy. The flower petals floating on the waters have been scattered as offerings to the gods.

## How Hinduism began

Hinduism has its roots in an ancient civilization known as the Indus Valley Civilization. This flourished between 3500 and 1500BCE and is thought by some experts to have ended at about the same time that a nomadic people called the Aryans arrived in India. Hinduism developed from the religious ideas of both these peoples.

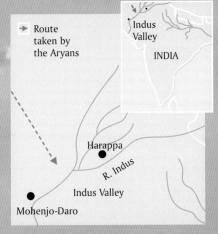

This map shows the route taken by the Aryan people when they arrived in India.

What is known about the Aryans comes mainly from a collection of hymns known as the *Vedas*. Knowledge about the religion of the Indus Valley People comes mainly from finds made at the cities of Harappa and Mohenjo-Daro.

Archaeological finds, like this statue of a priest king found in Mohenjo-Daro, have given experts valuable clues about the religion of the Indus Valley People.

## A varied religion

Hinduism was not founded by an individual person, and it developed slowly, over a long period of time. For these reasons it is a very varied religion. The story below gives some idea of its variety.

*A "mysterious beast" (actually an elephant) came to the Land of the Blind. The king sent his courtiers to find out what it was.*

*"The beast is like a wall,"* said one man, stroking the elephant's side.

*"I think it's like a spear,"* said a second man, as he touched its tusk.

*"I think it's like a fan,"* said a third man, as he explored its ear.

*"I think it's like a tree,"* said a fourth man, as he leaned against its leg.

*"I think it's like a snake,"* said a fifth man, as he tickled its trunk.

*"I think it's like a rope,"* said the sixth man, as he tugged its tail.

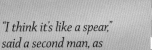

All the men were right, but only in part; they were telling a part of the whole truth. Like the elephant, Hinduism too is made up of very many different parts. For many Hindus, though, beneath all the variety there is one unchanging reality. This is called Brahman.

Hindus use complex patterns like this one in worship. It draws your eye toward the middle, which signifies Brahman.

## Brahman

Brahman most commonly refers to an unchanging ultimate reality which many Hindus believe exists beyond the ever-changing, everyday world of appearances.

Legend has it that a wise man taught his son about Brahman by asking him first to put some salt into water and then to take it out again. Of course, the salt dissolved and the son could not take it out. His father told him that the presence of Brahman in the world is like the salt in the water: invisible but everywhere.

This is the sacred symbol and sound "Aum" or "Om". There are many explanations of its meaning, and they all lead to Brahman.

## The soul

Hinduism teaches that each living being has a soul, called Atman. Some Hindus believe that Atman (the individual soul) is part of Brahman (the universal soul). Others see Atman and Brahman as distinct and separate things.

INTERNET LINKS

For links to websites where you can find out more about Hinduism, see pictures of Mohenjo-Daro and read more about Brahman, go to **www.usborne-quicklinks.com**

13

Hinduism has thousands of gods and goddesses. Each god or goddess has his or her own special characteristics. Hindus usually worship the gods and goddesses of their choice. Many Hindus believe that all these different deities are in fact different aspects of the same unchanging ultimate reality – the supreme Brahman.

## The Hindu trinity

Three Hindu gods – Brahma, Vishnu and Shiva – are associated with the creation, preservation and destruction of the world. This cycle of creation, destruction and re-creation is thought to happen eternally; it has no beginning or end.

Brahma (not to be confused with Brahman) is the creator. Vishnu is the preserver and Shiva is the destroyer. Shiva is also known as the liberator because it is through destruction that re-creation is possible. Together, these three are known to Hindus as the trinity, or *Trimurti*, meaning "three forms".

Brahma has four heads and sees in all directions. The statue sitting on the left of the main picture is Brahma.

Vishnu, the preserver of the universe, is said to have come down into the human world in various physical forms, known as *avatars*. For example, he came down first as Matsya, the fish, and then as Kurma, the tortoise. As the seventh and eighth *avatars*, Rama and Krishna, Vishnu walked on Earth in human form.

Varaha, the boar, is the third *avatar* of Vishnu.

The tenth and last *avatar* has not yet appeared. It is said that at the end of the present age, Vishnu will come to Earth as Kalki, riding a white horse, to destroy the wicked and re-establish order.

Statues of gods and goddesses adorn many Hindu temples. The scene below, from the Sri Murugan Temple near Hampi, in India, shows the wedding of Devayanai and Muruga.

Rama and his wife, Sita, represent an ideal couple. They are respected for their purity of character, their love for each other and their high moral values. One story tells how Sita was kidnapped by Ravana, the demon king of (Sri) Lanka. Helped by the monkey-god, Hanuman, Rama defeated Ravana and rescued Sita. This victory is seen by many Hindus as the triumph of good over evil.

The god Rama. Tales of Rama and Sita are told in a book called the *Ramayana*.

Parvati, wife of Shiva

Saraswati, goddess of learning, wife of Brahma

Lakshmi, goddess of wealth and beauty, wife of Vishnu

Devayanai, the daughter of Indra

Krishna is perhaps the most popular of the *avatars* of Vishnu. Different people who worship Krishna focus on different aspects of his personality. Some dwell on his innocence and charm as a child, others on his many pranks as a young cowherd, and his pure love for a milkmaid named Radha. Yet others admire his wisdom as a warrior and king.

Krishna is usually pictured with blue skin. As in this illustration, he is often shown playing the flute.

Shiva, the destroyer or liberator, is often shown as an awesome figure, with four arms, matted hair, a crescent moon on his head and a snake twined around his neck.

This statue shows Shiva dancing. The hoop of flames around him represents the energy of the universe and its creatures.

Shiva's upper right hand is sometimes shown holding a drum on which he beats out the rhythm of his dance: the dance of liberation and re-creation. Shiva has a third eye in the middle of his forehead. It symbolizes many things, including his wisdom.

can find out more about Hinduism, learn more about Hindu gods and goddesses and discover the different forms of Vishnu, go to **www.usborne-quicklinks.com**

## Parvati, Durga and Kali

Three goddesses are associated with Shiva. Parvati, his beautiful and gentle wife, matches the compassionate side of Shiva's nature. Durga and especially Kali are fierce and powerful: a match for Shiva's destructive side. Durga, the Inaccessible, slays demons with a sword. Kali is known as a destroyer of evil.

Parvati

## Ganesha

Ganesha, a son of Shiva and Parvati, is thought to remove obstacles. For this reason people often worship him at the beginning of a new undertaking such as at the start of a journey or at a wedding. One story tells how Shiva beheaded Ganesha in a fit of anger. Later Shiva restored Ganesha to life by giving him an elephant's head.

The statue at the bottom right of the main picture is Ganesha. With his big ears he can listen to everyone's prayers. His pot-belly represents wealth and success.

Indra, the god of rain, storms and battle

Muruga, one of the sons of Shiva and Parvati

Vishnu, sustainer of the universe

Shiva

## Hindu sayings

Here are a few sayings from Hinduism. The names of the people who said them or the scriptures from which they are taken are written after each one.

*As a man casts off his
worn-out clothes
And takes on other new
ones in their place
So does the embodied soul
cast off his worn-out bodies
And enters others new.*
                    Krishna in the Bhagavad Gita

*From the unreal lead me to the real,
from darkness lead me to light, from
death lead me to immortality.*
                    Brihadaranyaka Upanishad

*Real happiness of heart cannot be
attained without giving up the ideas
of "I" and "mine".*
                    Tulsidas

*I have now come to a stage of
realization in which I see that God
is walking in every human form and
manifesting Himself alike through the
sage and the sinner, the virtuous and
the vicious. Therefore when I meet
different people I say to myself, "God
in the form of the saint, God in the
form of the sinner, God in the form
of the righteous, God in the form
of the unrighteous."*
                    Ramakrishna

*Earth has enough for everyone's need
but not for everyone's greed.*
                    Mahatma Gandhi

## Endless cycle

Hindus believe that living things do not have just one life, but are all trapped in an endless cycle of life, death and rebirth. This cycle is called *samsara*. *Samsara* is seen as difficult and pointless, and Hindus hope eventually to be freed from it. It is symbolized by a wheel, known as the wheel of life. This wheel of life is kept spinning by *karma*, or action.

The wheel
of life

## Actions

*Karma* refers to a person's actions, good or bad. Every action shows results in this life and the next. Good actions lead to a better life the next time, and bad actions lead to a life of suffering. Hindus believe that very bad actions can result in a person's rebirth not as a human being, but as an animal or insect. This means that it becomes much more difficult to gain the knowledge needed to escape *samsara*.

This is part of a seventeenth-century illustration of a scene in the Hindu sacred text, the *Ramayana*. It shows the monkey-god Hanuman before Rama's wife, Sita.

## Release

Release from the cycle of rebirth and suffering is called *moksha*. People can hope to achieve *moksha* only by striving to replace their ignorance with wisdom. What prevents people from doing this is *maya*. *Maya* is illusion, as shown in the story below.

*A man thought he saw a
snake in the corner of his
room, coiled up and ready
to strike. He panicked
and ran away.*

*The man rushed around,
warning other people not
to go near the snake.*

*If only he'd looked more
closely at the "snake",
he'd have seen that it
was just a harmless
piece of old rope.*

What people don't notice when looking at the world around them is the way it really is beneath the surface. For many Hindus the only reality is Brahman. The rest is illusion.

## Sacred writings

All the sacred books mentioned on this page were written in Sanskrit, the language of ancient India. Nobody knows exactly when they were compiled, as it was so long ago. All are believed to have been written before the Common Era, some over a period of several centuries.

तत्त्वं असि

"That thou art" in Sanskrit, a phrase repeated in the *Upanishads*, underlines the harmony between Atman and Brahman.

The *Vedas* were passed on by word of mouth for centuries before being written down. The oldest and most sacred of the four *Vedas* is the *Rig Veda*. It contains a wide range of subjects, including tales of the world of the deities.

The *Mahabharata* has over 100,000 verses and is probably the world's longest poem. It tells of the life-long strife between two lines of princes of a royal family, resulting in a war in which one line is destroyed.

The *Upanishads* consist of philosophical discussions which teach about Brahman and the various ways to achieve *moksha*.

The *Ramayana* tells the life story of Rama and Sita (see page 14). It is believed to have been first written by a man named Valmiki.

### INTERNET LINKS
For links to websites where you can learn more about the basic teachings of Hinduism, and read stories from its sacred books, go to **www.usborne-quicklinks.com**

## Place in society

The Hindu scriptures contain guidelines on how the four ancient social groups in India should work in harmony. These groups were known as *varnas*. The first *varna* consisted of priests and teachers, known as *Brahmins*. Rulers and soldiers, called *Kshatriyas*, made up the second *varna*. The third contained merchants and farmers. They were called *Vaishyas*. Members of the fourth *varna* were *Shudras*. They were manual workers.

Rather than these four *varnas*, what can be seen in Hindu society today are thousands of groups called castes, or *jatis*. A person is born into a caste. Differences between castes are not as rigid as they were in the past, but caste is still important in defining a Hindu's place in society.

### Stages of life

The scriptures also describe four stages of life, called *ashramas*. These are the student, the family man, the recluse, and the wandering holy man who cuts all family ties, owns nothing and lives by begging. The ultimate spiritual goal for a Hindu is to achieve *moksha* and to be united with Brahman.

These people are *sadhus* – Hindu wandering holy men. They have made a pilgrimage to Varanasi, in India, and are sitting on the steps that lead down to the River Ganges.

The *ashramas* provide a path toward that goal, by helping people break free from attachments to things in life, but in reality they exist more in theory than in practice.

### Duty

Hindus try to live according to *dharma*. This is a duty or particular way of behaving which governs a person's life. *Dharma* is determined by a person's position in society (*varna*) and by the stage of life reached (*ashrama*).

### Important life events

The most important stages in a Hindu's life, such as birth and death, are marked by rituals and celebrations called *samskaras*. They all take place in front of a sacred fire. There are 16 *samskaras* in all. Three of these take place before a baby is born.

## Birth customs

Soon after birth, a Hindu baby is washed and the holy word "Aum" is written on the tongue with a golden pen dipped in honey. Ten days later, the baby is named at a ceremony called the *namakarana*. At this point, the baby's horoscope is cast. This is a chart showing the position of stars and planets when the baby was born. The chart is used later in life, for example, to decide on the best date for ceremonies such as coming of age or a wedding.

The simplified North Indian style Hindu horoscope below represents the heavens. It has 12 sections or "houses". Each house represents particular aspects of life, such as health or happiness. Hindus believe that the positions of the Sun, Moon and planets in the houses influence a person's life.

There are other *samskaras* to mark certain childhood events. These include the first time a baby is taken outside to see the Sun, the first meal of solid food, and the first haircut.

## Coming of age

Between the ages of eight and twelve, Hindu boys have a coming of age ceremony called the *upanayana*. This shows that the boy is thought old enough to find out more about his religion. In the past, *upanayana* was meant to be the initiation ceremony to the study of the scriptures in Sanskrit. These days, it is more usual for a boy just to learn some prayers.

A priest blesses a long, white cotton thread and places it over the boy's left shoulder and under his right arm. The thread has three strands, to remind the boy that he has a debt to god, to his ancestors and to his spiritual teacher. The strands also stand for the three Hindu gods, Brahma, Vishnu and Shiva. The boy wears the sacred thread for the rest of his life.

## Hindu weddings

Most Hindu marriages are arranged by the couple's parents. The wedding ceremony can last for up to 12 days, and can take place anywhere. The exact form of the ceremony may vary, but all share some common rituals. The bride and groom do all the rituals with the help of a priest. They make vows of loyalty and sharing in front of a sacred fire, which is seen as a holy witness.

The bride's red sari is tied to the groom's garment to symbolize their marriage. The bride and groom then walk around the fire, reciting prayers and hymns.

This illustration from a seventeenth-century Indian manuscript shows a bride and groom being prepared for their wedding.

The bride steps three times on a grinding stone as a sign that she will be steadfast and loyal to her husband and his family. The couple may also take seven steps around the fire. Each step is a symbol of an aspect of their life together, such as wealth or children.

## Death customs

Hindus believe that after a person has died, the soul comes back in another form. It is thought that dying close to the River Ganges may save a person from many rebirths and so bring them closer to *moksha*. A dying person who can't get to the River Ganges may be given water from it to drink.

According to Hindu teaching, a person's body is no longer needed after death. For this reason, Hindus burn, or cremate, their dead. In India, the body is placed on a pile of logs and the eldest son lights the fire. Three days later, the ashes are collected and placed in a river, ideally the River Ganges.

Hindus living in other countries may be cremated in a building called a crematorium rather than on a fire. It is common for relatives to send or take their ashes to the River Ganges to be scattered on its sacred waters.

INTERNET LINKS
For links to websites where you can find out more about rituals and customs in Hindu society, go to **www.usborne-quicklinks.com**

## Worship

Worship, known as *puja*, may take place in a temple or in the home. *Puja* at home tends to bring together the whole family. It takes place before the family shrine. Like the shrine shown on the right, this is usually decorated with pictures and statues of the deities. The family members light a lamp and pray together each day at the shrine.

Different Hindus may pray to different deities, depending on their family background and personal preferences. For many Hindus, worship of these deities helps to focus the mind and take them beyond the individual gods toward an understanding of Brahman. Many objects in the shrine appeal to the five senses of sight, hearing, smell, taste and touch, so involving the whole person in the worship.

By focusing on a *yantra*, or *mandala*, like this one, the meditator's concentration is drawn toward the point at the middle of the interlocking triangles. This point signifies Brahman.

A picture and a small statue of a god and goddess. This painting shows the goddess Lakshmi. The statue is of the god Krishna, with his flute.

Offerings of incense and flowers are placed in front of the images in the family shrine.

The scent of the incense fills the room as a reminder that Brahman is everywhere.

Prayer beads

Lamps called *diyas*

The bell is rung to help focus the mind during worship.

Food offerings, called *prasad*, are placed in the shrine. The family shares this food after worship.

This metal object represents the sacred word "Aum" or "Om", a sound-symbol, or *mantra*, for Brahman. It is said over and over again. There may also be singing.

## Yoga

Many Hindus use *yoga* and meditation to help them in their search for *moksha*. *Yoga* often involves extreme self-discipline, and the performance of complex physical and mental exercises to gain control over the body and mind. The different *yoga* postures are called *asanas*. There are different types of *yoga*, such as *Raja yoga* and *Hatha yoga*. Each type has its own unique approach to disciplining the mind and body.

In Hinduism, the term *yoga* is also understood in a second way. This refers to the different paths a Hindu can take toward *moksha* and union with Brahman. There are three such paths, which are shown below.

*Karma yoga is the discipline of action. People fulfil their dharma, for example by working hard to help others.*

*Bhakti yoga is the discipline of devotion. It means offering wholehearted love and prayer to a chosen deity.*

*Jnana yoga is the discipline of knowledge. Jnana means "wisdom". This type of yoga involves study and meditation.*

This holy man is sitting in a *yoga* posture called the lotus (*padma*) *asana*.

## Temples

There are no strict rules about when Hindus should go to the temple. Many choose to go on particular holy days and festivals. At other times, they visit the temple and take part in temple rituals only when they please.

Most temples are dedicated to a particular god or goddess. Usually a statue of the deity, called a *murti*, is kept in a shrine in the innermost part of the temple. During worship, Hindus walk clockwise around the shrine. Through *darshana*, or direct eye contact with the *murti*, Hindus believe that they can communicate with the god, and make special requests or gain spiritual insights.

Hindus may bring offerings such as fruit and flowers. Each temple has a *Brahmin* priest, who places the offerings before the deity to be blessed. The blessed offerings are later given back to the people, so bringing the deity's blessing to them. The priest may also make a mark of blessing, called a *tilaka*, with red powder on a person's forehead.

## Places of pilgrimage

Each year, millions of Hindus make pilgrimages, called *yatras*, to holy places. Although Hindus don't have to make these pilgrimages, many choose to do so because they feel it brings them closer to *moksha*. Hindu pilgrim sites are linked with deities or religious events and include various cities, rivers and mountains.

Hindus believe that temples are the homes on Earth of gods and goddesses. Many temples, like this one in India, are very ornate.

The most sacred of all Hindu pilgrimages takes place every 12 years, at the *Maha* (Great) *Kumbh Mela* festival. Millions of pilgrims come to the city of Allahabad, on the banks of the River Ganges, to bathe in the river. They believe that the water will wash away their sins. In 2013, over 80 million people came to *Kumbh Mela*.

**INTERNET LINKS**

For links to websites where you can learn more about Hindu forms of worship, and see pictures of temples, go to **www.usborne-quicklinks.com**

## The Hindu year

There are 12 months in the Hindu calendar. They are lunar months, which means that they are based on the phases of the Moon. Hindus use this calendar to calculate the dates of festivals and other religious events, as well as to cast horoscopes. In their everyday life, Hindus use the same calendar as everyone else.

There are hundreds of religious festivals held each year. Most are related to events in the lives of the deities. Some festivals, such as *Diwali*, are celebrated by Hindus worldwide; others are local.

The calendar above shows the main festivals of the Hindu year.

**JANUARY** — MAGHA — **FEBRUARY**
**DECEMBER** — PUSHYA
PHALGUNA — **MARCH**
MARGASHIRA
CHAITRA
**NOVEMBER**
**APRIL**
KARTIKA
VAISHAKHA
**OCTOBER**
**MAY**
ASHVINA
JYESHTHA
**SEPTEMBER**
**JUNE**
BHADRAPADA
ASHADHA
**AUGUST** — SHRAVANA — **JULY**

*Vasanta Panchami*: festival of Saraswati, and the coming of spring

*Holi*: spring festival

*Shivarati*: festival of Shiva

*Ramanavami*: the birth of Rama

*Diwali*: the festival of lights. For many Hindus the new year starts from this midnight.

*Hanuman Jayanthi*: the birth of Hanuman

*Navaratri*: festival of the Great Mother goddess Devi

*Dassehra*: death of Ravana

*Naga Panchami*: festival of snakes

*Rath Yatra*: feast of Lord Jagannath, one of the names of Krishna

*Ganesha Utsav*: the birth of Ganesha

*Janamastami*: the birth of Krishna

At the *Gangaur* festival in northwest Delhi, people gather to pray to richly-dressed statues of Shiva and Parvati.

## Diwali

*Diwali* is a five-day festival that takes place between October and November. It is a time when Hindus worship Lakshmi, the goddess of wealth and beauty. The festival also celebrates the triumphant return from exile of Rama, accompanied by his wife Sita. *Diwali* marks the beginning of the new Hindu year.

A *diya*

The name *Diwali* comes from the Sanskrit word *Dipavali*, which means "lights". Light represents knowledge, and the triumph of good over evil. *Diwali* is often known as the "festival of lights". Houses and temples are decorated with small clay lamps called *diyas*, and people set off fireworks to drive away the darkness, and to light the path home of Rama and Sita.

Before *Diwali*, houses are cleaned thoroughly then decorated for the festival. It is thought that Lakshmi will enter a clean and beautiful house, and bless those who live there. *Diwali* is a time for putting on new clothes, visiting relatives and exchanging cards, presents and sweet foods.

In some places, people paint geometric designs, called *rangoli* patterns, on the ground outside their homes for *Diwali*.

# Holi

*Holi* marks the beginning of spring. It commemorates the death of Holika, a wicked woman whom legend says tried to kill her nephew for being a follower of Krishna. On the night before *Holi*, huge bonfires are lit and models of Holika are burned. On the day of *Holi* itself, people remember the pranks that Krishna, as a cowherd, used to play on the milkmaids. There are processions, singing and dancing, and people throw powdered dyes and water over each other. At *Holi*, people take the opportunity to visit and greet each other.

## Shivarati

Shiva's festival is *Shivarati*. It falls in March at the New moon, which is the night when the Moon can't be seen from the Earth. Many people eat nothing all day, and only break this fast the next morning, having stayed awake all night to pray to Shiva.

Shiva

## Dassehra

The festival of *Dassehra*, between September and October, remembers Rama's victory over the giant Ravana (see page 14). Key moments from the life of Rama and Sita are retold in dances and plays. Huge models of Ravana, stuffed with hay and firecrackers, are built. A person dressed as Rama shoots a flaming arrow at the model to set it alight.

A model of Ravana

(see page 14)

INTERNET LINKS

For links to websites where you can find out more about the Hindu year and its festivals, go to **www.usborne-quicklinks.com**

# Navaratri

*Navaratri* is a nine-day festival between September and October during which Hindus worship different aspects of the Great Mother goddess, Devi. Some people fast for the whole nine days, or eat nothing but fruit and milk dishes. Some others choose to fast only on the eighth or ninth day.

In certain regions, it is the custom on the eighth or ninth day to choose nine girls to represent different aspects of Devi. These girls are treated as the goddess: their feet are ceremonially washed and people make offerings of food to them.

At *Holi*, Hindus throw powdered dyes and water over each other in memory of the mischievous tricks of Krishna. These boys are taking part in the festivities.

# JUDAISM

The history of the Jews goes back about 4,000 years, making their religion, Judaism, the oldest religion based on a belief in one God. Jews are born into their faith. Traditionally, anyone born of a Jewish mother is ethnically Jewish, whether or not they observe Jewish religious practices. Nearly half of the world's estimated 14 million Jews live in the USA, a quarter in Israel and the rest are scattered throughout the world.

The Western Wall in Jerusalem is one of the remaining parts of an ancient Jewish temple destroyed by the Romans in 70CE. Jews travel from around the world to visit Jerusalem and The Wall. They stand in front of it and say personal prayers to God.

# Chosen people

Jews trace their history back to a group of people called the Hebrews, who lived in what is now the Middle East. They were a nomadic people, which means that they didn't have a permanent home but moved from place to place.

One Hebrew, Abraham, is seen as the father of the Jewish people. He championed the main belief of Judaism – the idea of one God – at a time when others chose to worship many gods. Jews believe that God made a promise, called a covenant, to Abraham, in which God chose the Hebrews to be his special people, with a responsibility to keep all his commandments.

Abraham hears God's voice.

Jewish scriptures tell how Abraham and his elderly wife, Sarah, longed for children. One night, Abraham was told by God that he would have as many descendants as there were stars in the sky and that they would live in a land of their own: the Promised Land.

Soon after this, Abraham's son, Isaac, was born. Later, Isaac had a son, Jacob, whom God named Israel, and the descendants of Abraham became known as the Israelites. In the covenant God promised to care for the Israelites if they obeyed him.

## INTERNET LINKS

For links to websites where you can discover more about Jewish history and the laws of Moses, go to **www.usborne-quicklinks.com**

# The Exodus

In about 1250BCE, the Israelites were freed from Egypt, where they were slaves. This event, known as the Exodus, is very important in the history of Judaism. According to Jewish writings, God chose a man named Moses to plead with the Egyptian pharaoh (king) to free the Israelites. When Pharaoh refused to listen, God sent a series of ten plagues.

The final plague killed all the firstborn sons of the Egyptians and Pharaoh gave in. The Israelites started their journey but Pharaoh changed his mind and sent his army in hot pursuit. When the Israelites reached the Red, or Reed, Sea the waters miraculously parted, making a way for them. However, as soon as Pharaoh's army began to cross, the waters closed up and all his horses and men drowned.

Frogs were the second plague.

# God's laws

After the Exodus, the Israelites lived in the desert. During this time, God renewed the covenant with them and gave them a set of laws: the Ten Commandments. There are 613 Jewish laws, but these ten are the most famous.

### The Ten Commandments

1. *I am the Lord your God. Worship no god but Me.*
2. *Do not make or worship images.*
3. *Do not use God's name for evil purposes.*
4. *Observe the Sabbath (holy day).*
5. *Respect your father and mother.*
6. *Do not kill.*
7. *Do not be unfaithful in marriage.*
8. *Do not steal.*
9. *Do not accuse anyone falsely.*
10. *Do not envy things that belong to other people.*

This tenth-century *Bible* illustration shows Pharaoh's army drowning in the Red Sea, after the Israelites have crossed safely.

The man holding the staff is Moses.

## The Promised Land

About forty years after the Exodus, the Israelites reached a place called Canaan. God told them that this was the Promised Land. Two hundred years and many battles later, Canaan became an Israelite kingdom. King David is believed to have established a capital city at Jerusalem in around 993BCE. David's son, King Solomon, built a temple (which was later called the First Temple) in Jerusalem and this became the main focus for Israelite worship.

## The prophets

Once the Israelites became settled in Canaan, they did not always keep faithfully to God's laws. The prophets were people who reminded the Israelites of their promise to God and warned them of what would happen if they disobeyed these laws. The prophets were also often champions of the poor and needy, arguing that the Israelites should be more responsible toward others because of their covenant with God.

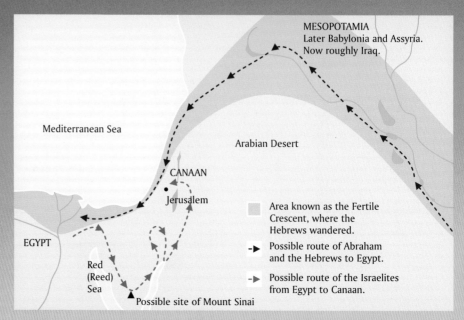

This map shows the area of the Middle East lived in by the Hebrews and later the Israelites.

The prophet Isaiah is shown in this Italian mosaic. He is believed to have lived during the seventh or eighth centuries BCE.

## Exile in Babylon

From the mid eighth century BCE onward, Canaan, by that time known as Israel, was ruled by many different peoples. These included the Assyrians, the Babylonians, and the Romans. In 586BCE, the First Temple in Jerusalem was destroyed by the Babylonians, and many Israelites were taken into captivity in Babylon. Jerusalem was in an area of Israel called Judah and the exiled Israelites became known as Jews.

## Exile in Europe

By the first century BCE, Israel was under Roman rule. In 70CE, after a Jewish rebellion, the Romans destroyed the Second Temple in Jerusalem. They also banned Jewish education and forced many Jews to leave Israel. The exiles joined existing Jewish groups around the Mediterranean. These groups eventually spread into eastern and central Europe.

The movement of Jews to various countries became known as the Dispersion. Today, communities of Jews living outside of Israel are said to be living in the Diaspora.

In order to preserve their identity, the Jews began to follow even more carefully the laws given to Moses. For instance, they were very strict about keeping their holy days and following certain food laws about what they could and could not eat. Outsiders did not understand these Jewish traditions and this led to suspicion and hatred.

## Messianic Age

All this time, the Jews were waiting for God to send a leader, or Messiah, who would re-establish a Jewish kingdom and begin an age of peace, called the Messianic Age. Christians believe that Jesus was the Messiah (see page 49) but Jews do not believe that the Messiah has arrived yet.

## The Middle Ages

In the centuries following the Diaspora, the Jews suffered further persecution, particularly by Christian rulers. One cause of their hatred was that Jews don't recognize Jesus as the Messiah.

The Jews were also accused of making money out of other people's debt. This came about because Christians were forbidden to lend money and charge interest on it, so this became a service provided by Jews, who were barred from entering many other professions.

In the Middle Ages, many Jews in Europe were forced to wear special clothes like these to single them out from Christians.

During the late Middle Ages, after years of ill treatment, Jews were expelled from England, France and Spain, where they had previously flourished. In countries where they were allowed to live, such as Italy, Germany and Austria, Jews were often forced to live in separate and inferior areas called ghettos.

INTERNET LINKS

For links to websites where you can find out more about the persecution of Jews and the Holocaust, and the history of modern Israel, go to **www.usborne-quicklinks.com**

## Persecution of Jews

Prejudice against Jews, called anti-Semitism, continued into the twentieth century and is still found in some countries today. Between 1871 and 1907, Russian, Polish and Lithuanian Jews were the victims of large-scale massacres, known as pogroms. Many Jews fled to the USA and some went to Palestine. (Palestine was the old land of Israel, renamed Palestine by the Romans.)

Nazis forced Jews to wear the yellow star of David.

The worst-ever persecution of Jews took place in World War II (1939-1945) and is known as the Holocaust. During this period, six million European Jews (over one third of the total world Jewish population) were rounded up and brutally murdered at death camps. This was carried out by the Nazis, who were in power in Germany under the leadership of Adolf Hitler.

## Modern Israel

During the nineteenth century, as Jews began to resettle in Palestine, a group called the Zionists started campaigning for a separate Jewish state to be set up there. After the Holocaust, this seemed important for Jewish survival. In 1948, Palestine was divided and the modern state of Israel was formed. Many Jews have since made Israel their home.

The creation of Israel led to tension between Israelis and non-Jewish Palestinians (mainly Muslim Arabs). There was also hostility between Israel and the surrounding countries, which were also mainly Muslim. Efforts to find a lasting solution to the conflict still continue today.

This sculpture in Jerusalem shows the agony and torture suffered by those who died in the Holocaust.

# Sacred writings

The *Tenakh* is a collection of 24 books, which are arranged in three main sections. The first five books are known as the *Torah* which means "teachings". These contain the instructions which God gave to Moses. The remaining 19 books are divided into the *Nevi'im* (eight books) and the *Ketuvim* (eleven books). These contain histories, poems, prophecies, hymns and sayings.

Although some of the material contained in the *Tenakh* was being passed on by word of mouth from around the time of Moses, the books themselves are thought to have been written down over about 900 years, from around 1000 to 100BCE. They were written mainly in the Hebrew language.

Copies of the *Torah* for use in worship at the synagogue are handwritten on parchment scrolls rather than printed in book form. This man is a *sofer* or scribe, who painstakingly copies out each word of the *Torah* by hand.

Tradition has it that God spoke the words of the *Torah* to Moses. Some modern scholars believe that the material came from various sources. Today, all of Jewish teaching is often referred to as the *Torah*.

Another set of writings, the *Talmud*, contains the thoughts on the *Tenakh*, of about 2,000 rabbis. A rabbi is an expert Jewish teacher.

The *Talmud* has two parts: the *Mishnah* and the *Gemara*. The *Mishnah* is a collection of writings about Jewish law, including laws on marriage and farming. The *Gemara* consists of comments about the *Mishnah*.

The *Midrash* is yet another important collection of writings. Many of the texts are in the form of stories which explain some aspects of the *Tenakh*.

## Two Jewish groups

Religious Jews are divided into two main groups: Orthodox and non-Orthodox. The differences between the groups can largely be seen in their everyday life as well as their worship.

This Orthodox Jewish father is showing his son how to prepare for worship.

As part of their morning worship, Orthodox Jews strap small boxes containing prayers around their head and around the arm nearest their heart. The boxes are called *tefillin* and the practice reminds Jews to worship God with head and heart.

One of the *tefillin* is worn on the head.

Jews also cover their head when praying as a sign of respect. Many Orthodox men wear a hat or a skull cap, called a *kippah*, all the time, as a sign of being always in God's presence.

Orthodox Jews accept the *Torah* and all its laws as being God's word to Moses, to be obeyed without question. Non-Orthodox Jews accept that human beings played a part in making the laws and so have tried to adapt Judaism to modern life. Non-Orthodox Jews are also known as Progressive, Liberal, Conservative, Reform or Reconstructionist Jews.

## Language

Jews have always learned to read ancient Hebrew because it was the language of the Israelites, and so they can read the prayers and scriptures in the synagogue. However, Hebrew as a living language had died out until the end of the nineteenth century, when Eliezer Ben-Yehuda, a Jewish settler in Palestine, decided to revive it. By refusing to speak anything else Ben-Yehuda began the development of modern Hebrew. This is slightly different from ancient Hebrew and is now Israel's official language.

Another Hebrew-based language, Yiddish, was spoken widely by East European Jews in previous centuries. It has now all but died out, and is spoken only by a group called the Chasidic Jews. Most Jews now speak the language of the country where they live.

## Jewish sayings

Below are just a few sayings from Judaism, with names of the people who said them or the scriptures from which they are taken.

*To everything there is a season, and a time to every purpose under the heaven.*
Torah

*Whether Jew or non-Jew, man or woman, rich or poor, it is according to deeds that God's presence descends.*
Talmud

*The more wealth, the more worry.*
Rabbi Hillel

*When God created the first man, He led him all around the trees in the Garden of Eden. God said to him:*
*"See my works, how beautiful and praiseworthy they are. Everything I have created has been created for your sake. Think of this, and do not corrupt it, there will be no-one to set it right after you."*
Midrash

*Do not limit a child to your own learning, for he was born in another time.*
Talmud

*He who meditates over words of Torah finds ever new meanings in them.*
Rabbi Shlomo ben Yitzchaki

### INTERNET LINKS

For links to websites where you can find out more about the *Torah*, Jewish faith and beliefs and the Hebrew language, go to **www.usborne-quicklinks.com**

## Places of worship

Jews go to a synagogue to worship, learn more about their faith and meet other people. The word synagogue means "a meeting place". Synagogues are normally rectangular buildings with seats on three sides. The fourth side faces Jerusalem.

## Jewish worship

Traditional services are less formal than those of many other religions. People may join or leave the worship at any time, and may talk to each other quietly during the service.

This rabbi (teacher of the faith) is reading from the *Torah* in a Progressive synagogue. She is helping the girl to prepare for her *bat mitzvah* ceremony (see page 32).

The service contains readings from the *Torah*, hymns (sacred songs) and prayers. Worship is often led by a rabbi (see below right) who may also give a talk about a reading from the *Tenakh*.

The Great Synagogue in Budapest, Hungary, is the second largest synagogue in the world. It is an important place of worship and also houses the Jewish Museum.

In Orthodox synagogues, men and women sit apart. The service is conducted in Hebrew, readings are chanted and no musical instruments are used. In Progressive synagogues, men and women sit together. Part of the service is conducted in the local language, and singing may be accompanied by an organ. The pictures below show some of the objects found in most synagogues.

*When not in use, the* Torah *scrolls are often covered with an embroidered cloth called a mantle.*

Torah *scrolls are kept in an ark – a cupboard or alcove on the synagogue wall that faces Jerusalem.*

*A light hangs in front of the ark to represent God's everlasting presence in the world.*

*The six-pointed star of David is a Jewish symbol. It is traditionally linked with King David.*

## Teachers of the faith

Teachers of the Jewish faith and law are known as rabbis. They aren't priests: for example, they don't act as a go-between for God and the people. However, like priests, rabbis conduct marriage and funeral ceremonies, give advice on spiritual matters and visit the sick. Women can become rabbis in non-Orthodox synagogues.

## Prayer

Prayer is an important part of the Jewish faith. Prayers can be said directly to God to praise Him, to give thanks, to ask Him for help or to confess sins.

There are written, formal prayers which have to be said at certain times. For example, there are set prayers that are spoken three times each day, prayers for the Sabbath (see right) and prayers for various festivals and fasts.

Before they go to sleep at night, many Jews say an important prayer called the *Shema*. Traditionally it is the first prayer that a Jewish child learns and the last prayer a Jew says before dying. One translation begins with, "Hear, O Israel, the Lord is our God, the Lord is One." The opening of the *Shema* written in Hebrew is shown below.

The opening words of the *Shema*

שמע ישראל
ה׳ אלהינו ה׳ אחד

There are written prayers for almost all aspects of Jewish life, from starting the day to surviving thunderstorms. Jews are also expected to say their own private prayers as they go about their daily lives.

INTERNET LINKS

For links to websites where you can discover more about Jewish synagogues, and the Sabbath, go to **www.usborne-quicklinks.com**

## The Jewish holy day

The Sabbath (*Shabbat* in Hebrew) is the Jewish holy day. It begins at sunset on Friday and lasts until sunset on Saturday. It is a day for rest and religious thought. No work is done because the Jewish creation story says that God made the world in six days, then rested on the seventh.

The family welcomes the Sabbath by lighting and blessing candles. Traditionally this is done by the woman of the house. People go to a service at the synagogue before eating a meal that was prepared before the Sabbath started. This meal is a family occasion with special songs, readings and a thanksgiving prayer. There are also services on Saturday and the Sabbath ends with a ceremony at home.

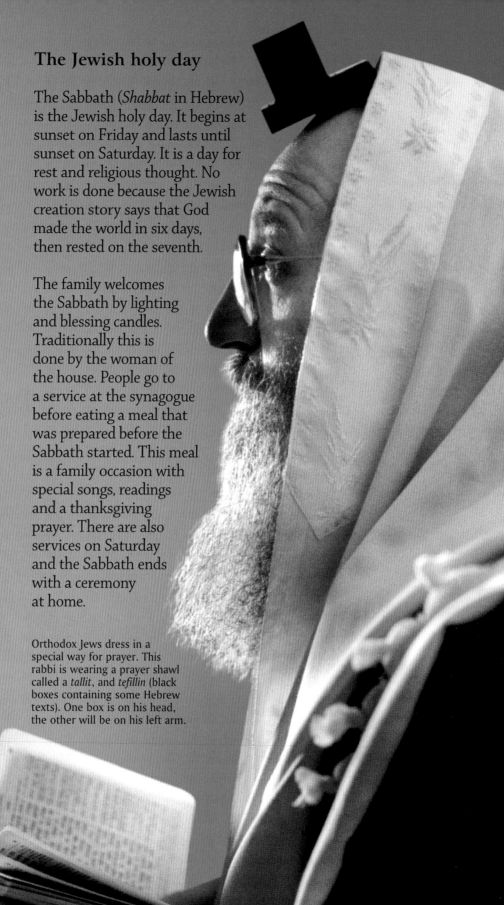

Orthodox Jews dress in a special way for prayer. This rabbi is wearing a prayer shawl called a *tallit*, and *tefillin* (black boxes containing some Hebrew texts). One box is on his head, the other will be on his left arm.

## The home

The Jewish home is even more important than the synagogue for making sure that the Jewish faith is continued. The ideas of community and family have become particularly important to Jews, partly because of the amount of persecution they have suffered over the years.

Traditionally, the mother has a very important role in keeping the faith alive. She is responsible for making sure that her family takes an active part in worship. She is also responsible for the preparations for religious festivals, such as Passover.

Most Jewish houses have small plastic, metal or wooden cases, called *mezuzahs* or *mezuzot*, attached to the doorposts. A *mezuzah* contains Hebrew texts from the *Torah*. It is placed on a doorpost as a reminder of the constant presence of God and God's commandments.

Every time Orthodox Jews pass through a door with a *mezuzah*, such as this one, on the doorpost, they will kiss their fingers and touch the *mezuzah*.

*Kosher* shops sell food that has been prepared following rules in the *Talmud*. This shop window is displaying scrolls and *matzah* – Jewish bread made without yeast for the Passover festival.

## Food laws

In Orthodox homes especially, food must be prepared in accordance with God's laws to make it *kosher* (fit). Meat and milk products must never be eaten at the same time or prepared with the same utensils. The *Torah* also forbids many foods, including pork and shellfish.

Meat must be drained of blood because the blood is seen as the life of the animal and so is too sacred to be eaten. Animals are slaughtered by a special method which is designed both to kill with the least amount of pain and to drain the blood.

## Birth customs

When a Jewish boy is eight days old, a ceremony called *Brit Milah* is held. At this ceremony, a small piece of skin (the foreskin) is cut from the baby's penis. This practice, which is known as circumcision, dates from the time of Abraham. It is done as a sign of the covenant between God and Abraham (see page 25), and it shows that the boy is a member of the Jewish people.

After the ceremony, the boy is blessed, prayers are said, and wine is drunk. He is then given his names. Jewish children have two names. One is a special, holy name, often in Hebrew. The other is an everyday name, usually from the country where they live.

A Jewish girl is taken to the synagogue, often on the first Saturday after her birth. At the service, her Hebrew name is announced to the congregation and she is blessed. In this way girls are welcomed into the faith.

## Coming of age

At the age of 13, a boy is considered to be an adult for religious purposes and is called *bar mitzvah*. This means "son of the covenant" or "son of duty". The event is marked by a ceremony in the synagogue, followed by a party. Progressive synagogues hold an equivalent ceremony called *bat mitzvah* ("daughter of duty") for girls when they reach the age of 12.

Jewish weddings can take place in a synagogue, in a home or outside. Many couples choose to have their wedding outside as a reminder of God's promise to Abraham that he would have as many children as there were stars in the sky (see page 25). The ceremony may vary depending on whether the service is Orthodox or Progressive.

The wedding begins with the signing of a contract called the *Ketubah*. This sets out the man's responsibilities to his wife. The main ceremony takes place under a *chuppah*, a cloth wedding canopy supported by four poles. It symbolizes the home the couple will make together. The rabbi blesses the marriage over a cup of wine and the groom gives the bride a plain gold ring.

Some Jewish couples are married under a prayer shawl, or *tallit*, held up by four poles. This couple is posing for their wedding photograph with a *tallit* draped over their heads.

When some Jews first hear of the death of a close relative, they make a tear in their clothes as a sign of grief. One way Jews cope with their grief is by believing that God shares their suffering.

Friends and family light a special candle in a glass holder and place it beside the dead person as a sign of respect. They stay with the body until the burial or cremation. Orthodox Jews always bury their dead but Progressive Jews may be cremated.

For the first week after a person's death, some families don't drink wine or eat meat, except on the Sabbath. Some also don't go to work or listen to music. Traditionally, the mourning period lasts for a month. During this time, the severity of the mourning rituals gradually lessens.

## INTERNET LINKS

For links to websites where you can learn more about Jewish birth and wedding celebrations, food laws and the observation of the Sabbath, go to **www.usborne-quicklinks.com**

## Jewish festivals

There are many Jewish festivals held throughout the year. Most of these are related to events that happened during the history of the Jewish people.

The Jewish calendar is based on the Moon's cycles and it is used to determine when festivals should be held. For everyday purposes, Jews use the calendar of the country in which they live. For Jews a day lasts from sunset to sunset, so all Jewish holidays begin on the evening before the date of the event.

## Jewish new year

The Jewish year begins in the month of *Tishri* (around September or October). Jews around the world celebrate the new year with a two-day festival known as *Rosh Hashanah*. Jews believe that on the first *Rosh Hashanah* God created the world and humans. They also believe that God begins to judge everyone at *Rosh Hashanah* and decides what will happen to them during the coming year.

This man is sounding a ram's horn or *shofar* at the festival of *Rosh Hashanah* to "wake" people so that they can prepare to lead better lives.

During *Rosh Hashanah*, Jews eat sweet foods such as honey cake. This represents their wish for a sweet year ahead. *Rosh Hashanah* begins a ten-day period of atonement (making amends). During this time, Jews pray, give to charity and ask for forgiveness to try to influence God's judgement and make the next year better for themselves.

## Day of Atonement

Ten days after *Rosh Hashanah* comes the Day of Atonement or *Yom Kippur*. This is the most sacred day in the year and services are held continuously from morning to evening. These include readings from the *Tenakh* and prayers asking for forgiveness. Between *Rosh Hashanah* and this day, Jews also seek forgiveness from people they have wronged during the year.

To help Jews to focus on their spirit at *Yom Kippur*, the *Talmud* forbids them to do certain physical things, as shown below.

*Yom Kippur is a day of fasting. Adult Jews, except those who are sick, don't eat or drink for the day.*

*On this day Jews are not allowed to wash themselves or put perfume, lotions or oils on their skin.*

*The Talmud also forbids the wearing of leather things on* Yom Kippur. *This includes items such as shoes and belts.*

## Passover

Passover, or *Pesach*, is held in March or April and lasts for eight days. It marks the escape of the Israelites from Egypt. The Jews believe that on the night before their escape, the angel of death, who was sent by God, "passed over" the houses of the Israelites while killing the eldest son of each Egyptian family. God had told the Israelites to smear lambs' blood on their doorposts as a sign to the angel to pass by.

Passover services are held in the synagogue, but the most important ceremony takes place at home. Before this, the house is spring-cleaned to remove every last trace of leavened bread (bread made with yeast). This is done because when the Israelites escaped from Egypt, there was no time for the bread to rise, as they had to leave as soon as they possibly could.

Once the cleaning is over, the main ceremony, called the *seder*, is held. This includes a meal in which some of the food and drink has special meaning.

A paste made from apples, nuts, wine and cinnamon symbolizes the bricks and mortar used by the Israelites to build Egyptian houses. A roasted lamb-bone is a reminder of what happened on the eve of the Exodus. The bitter taste of horseradish is a reminder of the misery of the slaves, and salt water symbolizes their tears. Sprigs of fresh parsley represent spring and new life, and an egg is also a symbol of new life.

Many Jews make pilgrimages to Jerusalem to celebrate *Sukkot*. The pilgrims in this photograph are holding a covered *Torah* scroll and blessing the four plants which are believed to symbolize the harvest given by God: *etrog* (citrus fruit) and *lulav* (date palm, myrtle and willow).

Unleavened bread (bread made without yeast) called *matzah* represents the flat bread that the Israelites took with them on the night of their escape.

The most important part of the ceremony is when the youngest child asks the ritual question: "Why is this night different from other nights?" In answer, the story of the Exodus from Egypt is read from a special prayer book called the *Haggadah*.

The egg, lamb-bone and other symbolic foods which form part of the traditional Passover meal are often presented on a special *seder* plate like this one.

## Other festivals

Other Jewish festivals include *Shavuot* and *Sukkot*. *Shavuot* celebrates the giving of the Ten Commandments to Moses. Jews often stay up all night studying the *Torah*. During the festival of *Sukkot* many Jews spend time living in temporary dwellings, called *sukkot*, made of wood and leaves. This is in remembrance of when the Israelites were wandering in the wilderness.

*Hanukkah*, the festival of lights, is held in November or December and lasts for eight days. It celebrates the Jewish rededication of the Temple in Jerusalem in 164BCE, after it had been wrecked and made unholy by Greek invaders. Each household lights candles in a nine-branched candlestick. A *shamash*, or servant candle, is used to light the others: one on the first night, two on the second, and so on, until all eight candles are burning.

┌INTERNET LINKS┐

For links to websites with more about Jewish festivals, go to **www.usborne-quicklinks.com**

# BUDDHISM

Buddhism was developed in India about 2,500 years ago by a man named Siddhattha Gotama. He became known as the Buddha, which means the "enlightened one". There are now over 500 million Buddhists. Most of them live in countries to the east of India, but the religion has also spread to Europe, the USA, Australia and New Zealand.

The founder of Buddhism, later known as the Buddha, grew up in a Hindu family. This young Buddhist monk is visiting a Hindu temple in Cambodia. His shaved head and orange robes are a sign that he has turned away from the everyday world, with its emphasis on wealth and possessions, and has dedicated his life to following the teachings of the Buddha.

## A time of change

At the time of Siddhattha Gotama's birth, many Hindus were looking for new answers to certain questions, especially questions about suffering. They wanted to know why people needed to suffer and how it could be avoided. This was a particularly serious problem for Hindus as their belief in rebirth meant suffering not just in one life but in many. Siddhattha became interested in the problem and set about finding new ways of solving it.

## Born a prince

Siddhattha was probably born in about 563BCE. His father was the ruler of a small kingdom in northern India, near what is now Nepal, and his family were Hindus. According to one legend, a fortune teller predicted that Siddhattha would be a great emperor, provided he did not see the four sights shown below.

A sick man

An old man

A dead man

A monk

If, however, he were to see these things, he would take up the life of a wandering holy man. Siddhattha's father wanted his son to rule after him, so vowed to keep him from such sights. Siddhattha lived in luxury at the palace, grew up kind and good, married and had a son. Just when his life seemed complete, he began to question the value of his idle, luxurious life. One day, he went outside the royal park and saw the four sights.

## The search

Siddhattha realized that even the most rich and powerful ruler cannot escape the suffering of illness, old age and death. He saw the fourth sight, the monk, as a sign that he should leave the palace and search for an answer to the problem of suffering. So, at the age of 29, he cut off his hair, put on beggar's robes and became a wandering holy man.

Siddhattha studied with some holy men but this did not lead him to an answer. He then followed a strict fast for six years. This left him exhausted and near death. He realized that the problem would not be solved by going to extremes and he vowed to adopt what he called the Middle Way: neither indulging in luxury, nor causing needless hardship to his body.

## Enlightenment

Tradition says that one evening, Siddhattha sat down in the shade of a banyan tree near a temple of the Hindu god Vishnu, at a place called Bodh Gaya in India. He stayed there all night, deep in meditation. Then, as dawn broke, he saw the meaning of all things unfold: he was enlightened. From this point on, Siddhattha was known as the Buddha.

*Sculptures of the Buddha often show him meditating, sitting with his legs crossed and his hands resting in his lap.*

## Nirvana

At the moment when he achieved enlightenment, the Buddha attained *nirvana*. This is freedom from the cycle of rebirth, and so freedom from suffering. Buddhists say that *nirvana* cannot be described in words; it lies beyond the definable.

The Buddha was also known as the *Tathagata*. This name means "Thus-gone" and describes someone who has achieved *nirvana*. Such a person is said to be totally free from the world and cannot be reborn. The Buddha went on to live until the age of 80.

*The Buddha is said to have lain on his side for his final entry into nirvana at death.*

INTERNET LINKS

For links to websites where you can you learn more about the life of the Buddha, and read stories about him, go to **www.usborne-quicklinks.com**

## The first teaching

After gaining enlightenment, the Buddha passed on his new-found knowledge to a group of monks. His first sermon took place in a deer park at Sarnath, near Benares (Varanasi) in India.

For the Buddha the need for an answer to the problem of suffering was too urgent to waste time in empty speculation. He did not try to answer the questions of whether God exists, or why and how the world was created. To do this, he said, would be like a man wounded by an arrow refusing to relieve his pain until he knew how many feathers the arrow had. Having the answers to such questions does not help to relieve the suffering.

The Buddha's main teaching was made up of what are known as the Three Universal Truths, the Four Noble Truths and the Eightfold Path. Together these are known as the *dharma*.

Buddhist monasteries are often built in remote and tranquil places, such as this one high up in the Himalayan mountains. There, the monks seek enlightenment through following the Buddha's teachings.

## The Universal Truths

1. Everything in life is impermanent and is constantly changing. The Buddha's thinking about this is similar to that of the Greek philosopher Heraclitus, who said that it is impossible for a person to step into the same river twice.

2. Impermanence leads to suffering. The fact that nothing remains the same makes life unsatisfactory. People desire and become attached to things which can't last. Even if someone achieves a state of contentment, it won't last. Indeed, knowing that the contentment must end is itself a source of suffering.

   To a Buddhist, suffering means not only the great pain and tragedies which people experience. It also means all those things which make life less than perfect.

3. There is no unchanging personal self. What people call the self is simply a collection of changing characteristics. The Buddha compared the self to a chariot, which is simply a collection of parts that are put together in a certain way but can be taken apart again.

This map shows some of the places that are associated with the Buddha's life.

## The Noble Truths

1. All life involves suffering.

2. The cause of suffering is desire and attachment.

3. Desire and attachment can be overcome.

4. The way to overcome them is to follow the Eightfold Path.

## The Eightfold Path

The Eightfold Path is the Middle Way followed by the Buddha in his own search for enlightenment. It is a code for living as a Buddhist.

1. Right viewpoint: for example, understanding the Noble Truths.

2. Right intention: for example, trying to act considerately.

3. Right speech: for example, avoiding anger, lies and gossip.

4. Right action: for example, living honestly and not harming living things. (Many Buddhists are vegetarians.)

5. Right work: avoiding jobs which harm anyone.

6. Right effort: for example, trying hard to overcome desire and attachment.

7. Right mindfulness: for example, thinking before speech or action.

8. Right meditation: freeing the mind of distractions, leading to enlightenment and *nirvana*.

An eight-spoked wheel is often used to represent the steps of the Eightfold Path.

## Sacred writings

At first, the Buddha's teachings were passed on by word of mouth. It was not until at least three centuries after his death that they were written down. One important collection of writings is called the *Tipitaka*, which means "three baskets". It was first written on palm leaves which were collected together in baskets. The *Tipitaka* contains the Buddha's sayings, comments on the sayings, and rules for monks.

**INTERNET LINKS**

For links to websites where you can find out more about Buddhist teachings, go to **www.usborne-quicklinks.com**

## Buddhist sayings

Below are some Buddhist sayings. The name of the person who said them or the scriptures from which they come are written underneath.

*It is you who must make the effort. The Great of the past only showed the way.*
Dhammapada

*There are two extremes which should be avoided:*
*1. Indulgence in sensual pleasures.*
*2. Indulgence in extreme hardship.*
Dhammacakkappavattama Sutra

*It is easy to see the faults of others, but difficult to see one's own faults. One shows the faults of others like chaff winnowed in the wind, but one conceals one's own faults as a cunning gambler conceals his dice.*
Dhammapada

*If you are afraid, you are in error. If you know how to calm your spirit and keep it still in all circumstances, you are in truth.*
Bodhidharma

*Go forth, O monks, for the good of the many, for the welfare of the many; out of compassion for the world teach this Dhamma which is glorious in the beginning, glorious in the middle and glorious at the end, in the spirit and in the letter.*
Vinaya Pitaka

*A state that is not pleasing or delightful to me, how could I inflict that upon another?*
Samyutta Nikaya

## The three jewels

Most Buddhists are united in their belief in the Buddha, the *dharma* (his teachings), and the monastic order of the *sangha* (see opposite). These are called the three jewels because they are so precious.

These Tibetan scriptures contain the Buddha's teachings, one of the three jewels of Buddhism.

## The five precepts

The Buddha taught that the way to enlightenment was for people to take responsibility for their own actions. He laid down five rules, or precepts, that every Buddhist should obey in everyday life.

1. *To avoid harming living things.*
2. *To avoid taking things that have not been freely given.*
3. *To live a decent lifestyle.*
4. *To avoid speaking unkindly or lying.*
5. *To avoid alcohol and drugs.*

## Meditation

In addition to obeying the five precepts, most Buddhists think that meditation is essential in achieving *nirvana*. It is through searching within the self during meditation that a person can come to understand the truth of the Buddha's teaching.

The basis for meditation is *samatha*. This is a peacefulness in which the mind is empty of all thoughts. A person can be helped to this calm state by concentrating on breathing or by focusing on an object such as a candle. Once the mind is quiet, a person may focus on the idea of impermanence and change. This stage is *vipassana*.

Many Buddhists believe that almost anything can be a focus for meditation. They talk of doing things in a mindful way. By this they mean concentrating only on the present moment and so not being distracted by conflicting thoughts. The pictures below show some things that can help people to meditate.

*People often sit with crossed legs or kneel on cushions.*

*They may offer flowers or incense to a statue of the Buddha.*

*The statue, or a candle or picture, may be used as a focus for meditation.*

*Closing the eyes and counting breaths helps them to be calm.*

## Rites of passage

Buddhism considers rites of passage less important than many other religions do. Some rites, such as birth or wedding ceremonies, are left mainly to local custom. This may be because Buddhists believe that attachment to self locks a person into a cycle of rebirth. It is not surprising therefore that the most celebrated events are those that lead a person to focus on the path to enlightenment.

When a person becomes a Buddhist, for example, there is, in most traditions, a short rite called a refuge ceremony. The person recites the three jewels:

*"I go to the Buddha for refuge.*
*I go to the dharma for refuge.*
*I go to the sangha for refuge."*

and the five precepts. Offerings of flowers and incense are made to a statue of the Buddha to show respect for him and his teaching.

## The sangha

*Sangha* is the name given to any community of Buddhist monks or nuns. The monks who heard the Buddha's first sermon at Sarnath were converted and formed the first *sangha*. At first, the Buddha was unsure whether to have women in the *sangha*. He was persuaded by his mother-in-law, who begged to join.

INTERNET LINKS

For links to websites where you can learn more about Buddhist monks and meditation, go to **www.usborne-quicklinks.com**

## Life in the sangha

Buddhist monks and nuns live in monasteries or nunneries. They live simply and own only eight items. These include three robes, a razor and a begging bowl. Local people often give food to the monks in return for a blessing.

Monks spend their time studying sacred texts, meditating, seeing to the day-to-day running of the monastery, and working in the community, for example, teaching, or caring for the sick. They have to obey a code of over 250 rules. These include the ten precepts, which are the five precepts obeyed by all Buddhists, plus another five (see right).

1. *To avoid eating too much, or eating after midday.*

2. *To avoid dancing and frivolous singing.*

3. *To avoid wearing adornments and perfumes.*

4. *To avoid sleeping too much, or in a soft bed.*

5. *To avoid handling gold and silver (money).*

## Pravrajya

It is the custom in certain Buddhist countries for boys to spend some time living as monks. The *pravrajya* ceremony, at which a boy becomes a novice monk, can take place from the age of eight. A boy may dress in fine clothes, before riding on horseback to the monastery. There, his head is shaved, he puts on plain robes and promises to obey the ten precepts.

Boys often dress in fine clothes for their *pravrajya* ceremony, as a reminder of the Buddha's life as a prince.

This boy has had his *pravrajya* ceremony. His head has been shaved to symbolize the removal of his past actions, and his readiness to start a fresh life.

In some *sanghas*, monks are allowed a few items in addition to the basic eight. These may include prayer beads, an umbrella, or a palm leaf fan, like the one the boy is holding here.

## How Buddhism spread

The first *sangha* spread the Buddha's teachings throughout northern India. Emperor Asoka, who ruled northern and central India from 269-231BCE, helped the religion to spread across India. He set up stone pillars carved with Buddhist teachings throughout his empire and sent missionaries into central Asia.

Asoka's son, Mahinda, took the religion to southern India and Sri Lanka, and it was carried east along trade routes into China. In many parts of India itself, Buddhism remained an active religion until at least 1200CE, when Muslim invaders destroyed many Buddhist temples, shrines and monasteries.

Soon after the Buddha's death, differences of opinion began to arise among his followers. These eventually developed into two types of Buddhism: Theravada and Mahayana.

Emperor Asoka helped Buddhism to spread across India and into central Asia.

To Afghanistan

JAPAN

CHINA

INDIA

The first *sangha* spread Buddhism in northern India.

Mahinda took Buddhism to southern India and Sri Lanka.

Buddhism was carried along trade routes into China.

Directions in which Buddhism spread

Theravada Buddhism

Mahayana Buddhism

To Indonesia and Borneo

This map shows the directions in which Buddhism spread from India to many other eastern countries, where it is still alive today.

These stone lions stood on top of one of the pillars set up by Emperor Asoka. The pillars were carved with Buddhist teachings.

## Theravada Buddhism

Theravada means "way" or "teachings of the elders". Theravada Buddhists believe that they follow the Buddha's original teachings more closely than other groups do.

A Theravada monk studying the teachings in the *Tipitaka*.

Theravada Buddhists look upon the Buddha as a remarkable person and a perfect model to imitate but believe that he was only human. When he died, he stopped being able to offer practical help to people still alive. For this reason, Theravada Buddhists do not pray to the Buddha. They believe that individuals must make their own way by following the teachings that were written down in the *Tipitaka*.

## Mahayana Buddhism

Mahayana Buddhists do not concentrate just on the Buddha Siddhattha Gotama. They see him as one of many Buddhas of the past, present and future. Also, they believe in *bodhisattvas*. This name means "Buddha-to-be". It describes people who are on the path to enlightenment and who have dedicated their whole spiritual career, over many lifetimes, to helping others toward the same state.

Mahayana Buddhists use the *Tipitaka*, and also other, more recent texts, called *sutras*. These are stories and parables which explain some parts of the Buddha's teaching that are difficult to understand. The most well-known are the *Diamond Sutra* and the *Lotus Sutra*. While the *sangha* is important, becoming a monk is not thought to be essential, and a person can seek *nirvana* while still being involved in society.

As Buddhism spread across Asia, Mahayana Buddhists adapted to the cultures they met. This led to the formation of distinctive branches of this type of Buddhism. Three of these are Vajrayana, Pure Land and Zen.

The Potala Palace, near Lhasa, in Tibet, is the official home of the Dalai Lama. It is an important place of pilgrimage for Vajrayana (Tibetan) Buddhists.

## Vajrayana Buddhism

Vajrayana Buddhism is also known as Tibetan Buddhism because it used to flourish in Tibet. Its leaders had political power as well as religious influence. Then, in the 1950s, Tibet was overthrown by China, a communist country which did not allow religion. Many Buddhists had to flee. The leader of Vajrayana Buddhism, who is called the Dalai Lama, still lives in exile in India.

## Pure Land Buddhism

Pure Land Buddhism began in China and spread to Japan in about the thirteenth century. The central figure is a Buddha known as Amida Buddha. He was so full of compassion that he took a vow that anyone calling on his name would be reborn in the Pure Land. This is a place in which it would be easy for everyone to follow the Buddha's teachings and reach *nirvana*.

## Zen Buddhism

Like Pure Land, Zen Buddhism began in China and spread to Japan in about the thirteenth century. Zen means "meditation" and Zen Buddhists try to spend as much time as possible being "mindful", or meditating on reality.

Zen Buddhists use painting, martial arts such as karate, and specially designed gardens to help them to focus their minds during meditation. They also use puzzles, called *koans*, such as this: what is the sound of one hand clapping? The purpose of *koans* is to challenge people's usual patterns of logical thought so that they see beyond the way they are used to thinking and so come to enlightenment.

Zen gardens provide a tranquil setting for meditation. The gravel is raked daily and represents constantly changing streams of water circling the permanent rocky islands.

### INTERNET LINKS

For links to websites where you can find out more about the different branches of Buddhism, and Zen meditation, go to **www.usborne-quicklinks.com**

43

## Holy places

Some of the main Buddhist pilgrimage sites are associated with important events in the Buddha's life: for example, the place of his birth (Lumbini Grove), his enlightenment (Bodh Gaya), his first teaching (Sarnath), and his death (Kusinara).

While on pilgrimage, Buddhists try extra hard to live according to the five precepts. They try to avoid behaving in a light-hearted way, and to keep their whole minds focused on their quest for enlightenment. Some walk barefoot, or crawl, for part of their journey. This is to show their understanding that suffering is part of life. Buddhists often walk around a pilgrimage site three times, symbolizing the three jewels.

The fifth-century stone stupa at Bodhnath in Kathmandu, Nepal is one of the largest in the world. Strings of prayer flags flutter from its spire, watched by the Buddha's all-seeing eyes.

## Places of worship

Many Buddhists visit temples or shrines to pay their respects to the Buddha and to meet and meditate with other Buddhists. Places of worship vary greatly, from vast, ornately decorated temples to a room in an ordinary building, that has been set aside for worship.

The oldest style of Buddhist shrine is called a *stupa*. The very earliest *stupas* were sealed mounds containing the Buddha's ashes. Later *stupas* were built to house copies of the Buddha's teachings and relics of later Buddhist teachers and *bodhisattvas*. Early *stupas* were simple mud-brick domes, but later ones were built from stone, and were often bell-shaped.

As Buddhism spread to China and Japan, the design of *stupas* changed, and taller, thinner buildings called *pagodas* were built. These are in the form of a tiered tower, often with eight sides. The number of tiers can range from three to thirteen, but it is always an odd number.

*This bell-shaped* stupa *houses a statue of the Buddha. Buddhists show their respect by walking three times around the* stupa.

Pagodas *are made of wood, brick or stone and are often topped with a mast. Many are decorated with paint or tiles; others are plain.*

## Buddhist rituals

Rituals are performed at a shrine in the home, as well as at a temple. The rituals may vary from one branch of Buddhism to another.

Offerings of flowers, candles and incense are often placed in front of a statue of the Buddha or a *bodhisattva*. This is done to show respect and because it is thought to encourage generosity. The flowers are a reminder that life on Earth is short. The candles symbolize enlightenment, and the scent of the incense represents the spread of the *dharma* throughout the world. Buddhists often lie face down on the floor in front of a statue or shrine as a sign of respect and thanks for the Buddha's teachings.

In Nepal and Tibet, prayers are sometimes written on flags. As the flags flutter in the breeze, the prayers are thought to be blown to all parts of the Earth.

Prayer is also important. In some religions, prayer is a way of asking or thanking a deity for something. Buddhists believe that prayer helps to join a person's inner thoughts with the forces of good.

As well as repeating short prayer phrases, called *mantras*, Buddhists in some countries use prayer wheels: cylinders with a paper scroll inside. Hundreds of *mantras* are written on the scroll. By spinning the prayer wheel, Buddhists believe that these *mantras* are released into the world. As the wheel spins, the *mantras* are repeated and become more powerful.

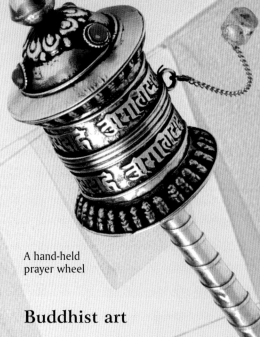

A hand-held prayer wheel

## Buddhist art

Buddhist art uses a wide variety of symbols to remind people of their beliefs. Every Buddhist temple has an image of the Buddha. The different positions of his body and hands have particular meanings. Many carvings and paintings show scenes and events from the Buddha's life. The Buddha himself is often represented by symbols, for example, an eight-spoked wheel, a banyan tree, a *stupa* and footprints.

Yet another common symbol in Buddhism is the lotus flower, which has its roots in mud at the bottom of ponds. The mud represents human life; the pure flower stands for enlightenment.

A lotus flower

**INTERNET LINKS**
For links to websites where you can take virtual tours of Buddhist holy places and find out more about Buddhist art, go to
**www.usborne-quicklinks.com**

## The Buddhist calendar

The Buddhist religious calendar is lunar, that is, based on the phases of the Moon. Buddhists say that the Buddha was born and died at a full moon and most festivals take place when the Moon is full.

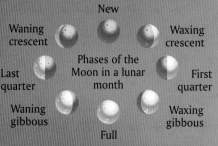

New

Waning crescent

Waxing crescent

Phases of the Moon in a lunar month

Last quarter

First quarter

Waning gibbous

Waxing gibbous

Full

There are many festivals during the year. Some are celebrated by Buddhists everywhere, others are only celebrated in a particular town or country.

## Buddha festivals

*Wesak* is the celebration of the Buddha's birth and, in Theravada countries, of his enlightenment and death too. It takes place at the full moon in late May or early June.

At this time, statues of the Buddha are decorated and, in China, bathed in scented water. People go to temples or monasteries to take offerings, meditate and hear a talk about the Buddha's enlightenment. Light has an important part to play in the *Wesak* celebrations. People light lamps, and there may be spectacular firework displays.

In Thailand this festival is called *Visakha*. At sunset, people walk in a lamp-lit procession to their local monastery. There they make offerings of flowers and incense, meditate, and walk three times clockwise around the shrine: once for each of the three jewels.

Candlelight symbolizes enlightenment.

In Japan, the Buddha's birth is celebrated at a spring flower festival called *Hana Matsuri*. There are fairs, with food stands, folk dancing and acrobats. Monks set up displays and models to remind people of the Buddha's birth story.

*Asala* Day commemorates the Buddha's first teaching. In Sri Lanka it is celebrated at the festival of the Sacred Tooth. A tooth, believed to be the Buddha's, is paraded through the streets in a golden casket.

Many Buddhists in western countries hold three separate festivals to celebrate the three jewels. These are Buddha Day, *Dharma* Day and *Sangha* Day.

Music often plays an important part in Buddhist festival celebrations. These Tibetan monks are playing a horn fanfare to greet the new year at the festival of *Losar*.

## Losar

*Losar* is a major Tibetan festival that takes place at the full moon in February. It celebrates the Buddha's early life and teaching, and also marks the beginning of the new year. Before *Losar*, people clean their homes as a sign of a fresh start. They carry lighted lamps through their homes, and set off fireworks. Monks put on bright costumes and masks, and dance to frighten away evil spirits.

Costumed dancers, like this one, act out the battle between good and evil at a Buddhist festival.

## Vassa

*Vassa* is a meditation retreat that takes place in the rainy season. In the Buddha's day, it was impossible to travel at this time, so he told the monks to stay in one place to study. All Buddhists try to put aside time for study and meditation during *Vassa*. At the end of the retreat, they give new robes to the monks.

## Obon

*Obon* is a Japanese festival held in July. It is a three-day celebration during which people pay their respects to family ancestors.

*Day 1.*
*People put fresh flowers and food offerings, such as cooked rice, on the family shrine to welcome their ancestors' spirits.*

*Day 2.*
*People put on their best clothes and enjoy a day of celebration, with feasting, processions, music and dancing.*

*Day 3.*
*People say goodbye to their ancestors, make offerings to the Buddha and ask him to bless them and their ancestors.*

## Uposatha Days

In addition to special festivals, every lunar month there are four *Uposatha* Days, when Buddhists perform their religious duties.

Some Buddhists fast on these days to show that they want to think about spiritual matters. They may visit their local temple or monastery, taking gifts and food for the monks. Buddhists believe that good deeds like this will make their lives happier, and will benefit others. If they don't achieve *nirvana* in this life, they believe that they will have a better life next time they are born.

### INTERNET LINKS

For links to websites where you can learn more about Buddhist festivals and special days, go to **www.usborne-quicklinks.com**

47

Part of Michelangelo's statue showing the death of Jesus on a cross (the crucifixion). Christians believe that Jesus is God's son, and see his death as proof of God's love for the world. As in this statue, Jesus is often shown with a serene expression on his face.

# CHRISTIANITY

Christians believe in the teachings of a man named Jesus, who was called Christ by his followers. Christ is the Greek word for "Messiah", meaning "anointed one". For Christians, Jesus is the Son of God: God in human form. Today Christianity is found in most parts of the world and, with 2.2 billion followers, it is the world's largest religion.

## Jesus' birth

Jesus was born a Jew in Roman-occupied Judea (an area which is now part of Israel) about 2,000 years ago. According to Christian scriptures, God sent an angel, Gabriel, to visit a young woman named Mary in the town of Nazareth. Gabriel told Mary that she would be the mother of Jesus. Christians believe that Mary was a virgin despite being a mother.

Jesus was born in the town of Bethlehem, where Mary and her fiancé, Joseph, had gone to pay their taxes. The town was crowded so they had to stay in a stable, which is where Jesus was born. One version of the story says that shepherds were the first to visit Jesus. In another version, wise men followed a star to the stable and gave Jesus three gifts.

This fifteenth-century Italian painting shows the humble birth of Jesus in a stable.

*Many Christians believe that the wise men's gifts have special meaning. The first gift was gold, symbolizing a king.*

*The second gift was a good quality incense called frankincense. This was a symbol of a holy man.*

*The final gift was a bitter incense called myrrh. This was used to anoint dead bodies, and so was associated with death.*

## The baptism of Jesus

Jesus grew up in Nazareth and probably became a carpenter. At about the age of 30, he asked his cousin, John, to baptize him in the River Jordan. Baptism involves being immersed in water as a sign of starting a new spiritual life. John recognized Jesus as the Messiah the Jewish people were waiting for (see also page 26).

John baptizing Jesus in the River Jordan

Scripture tells that the Spirit of God in the form of a dove came and rested on Jesus, while a voice from heaven said that he was God's Son. Christians believe that the name of Jesus also shows him to be the Messiah. In one version of the story, an angel came to Joseph while Mary was pregnant and told him to name the child Jesus. This is a version of the Hebrew name Joshua, meaning "God saves".

## Jesus' work

After his baptism, Jesus went into the wilderness for 40 days. While he was there, the devil (Satan) tried to tempt him but Jesus refused all the offers the devil made. This reminds Christians that believers can be tempted. After his time in the wilderness, Jesus chose 12 disciples (followers) and started teaching. He gained a reputation for healing sick people and performing miracles, for example feeding a crowd of 5,000 with only five loaves and two fishes.

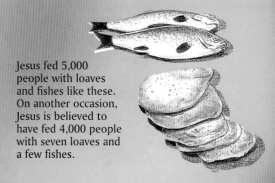

Jesus fed 5,000 people with loaves and fishes like these. On another occasion, Jesus is believed to have fed 4,000 people with seven loaves and a few fishes.

The Jewish religious authorities felt threatened by the popularity of Jesus, and by some of the things he and his disciples did. For example, Jesus made a point of helping social outcasts, non-Jews (known as Gentiles) and women. He also forgave sins, which the Jews believed only God could do.

┌─INTERNET LINKS─
For links to websites where you can find out more about the birth of Jesus, and learn about the basics of the Christian faith, go to **www.usborne-quicklinks.com**

## The teaching of Jesus

One of the most important sermons (talks) that Jesus gave is known as the Sermon on the Mount. In it, Jesus outlined his central teachings and he blessed groups of people, including the meek, the peacemakers and people who were being persecuted. He also described God's laws and said that people should obey them, for example, by loving their enemies and not judging others. The sermon included the Lord's Prayer which is still said today.

This thirteenth-century stained-glass window shows Jesus teaching in the synagogue. Jesus is shown with a halo. The disciples are wearing what medieval Christians thought of as Jewish hats, to emphasize that they were Jews.

Jesus said that people should repent of their sins (actions against God's laws) and make a fresh start. This was necessary before God's kingdom could be established. In God's kingdom, there would be justice and peace.

Jesus taught that love and serving others were more important than all the details of the Jewish law and he spoke of God as Father. At this time it was unheard of for anyone to speak of God in such a familiar way.

## The parables

Jesus often taught by telling parables – stories which teach a spiritual lesson. The parable known as the Good Samaritan is told below. It shows how people should help others, regardless of difference, for example, in race or beliefs.

*A Jewish man was on the road to Jericho when he was violently attacked by robbers and left for dead at the roadside.*

*A priest saw the man lying bleeding by the side of the road, but he hurried past without trying to help.*

*Like the priest, a second person also ignored the injured man and passed by without stopping.*

*A man from Samaria came along. Although Jews and Samaritans hated each other, he helped the man.*

## In Jerusalem

Three years after he began teaching, Jesus went with his disciples to the city of Jerusalem for the Passover festival (see page 35). Jesus arrived in Jerusalem riding on a donkey and many people welcomed him as a king. They hoped that he would overthrow the Romans and re-establish a Jewish kingdom. When they realized that this was not to be, the people turned against him.

## The Last Supper

Jesus shared the Passover with his disciples. During the meal, which became known as the Last Supper, he told them that he was about to die. He shared bread and wine with them, saying that the bread was his body and the wine was his blood, and that his followers should continue to share them in memory of him.

In many churches, Christians drink a sip of wine from a cup like this, called a chalice, in memory of the Last Supper.

## The crucifixion

Judas, one of the disciples, handed Jesus over to the authorities. Jesus was charged with blasphemy, which means treating God's name with disrespect.

Jesus was taken to the Roman governor, Pontius Pilate, who had the power to sentence people to death. Christian scriptures tell that Pilate was worried that the Jews might riot if he freed Jesus, so he gave in. He ordered Jesus to be crucified: fastened to a cross until he died. Two thieves were crucified with him, one on each side.

## The resurrection

Jesus was buried in a tomb, but on the third day after his crucifixion, the tomb was found to be empty. Some followers said that they had seen Jesus and the news quickly spread that he was resurrected (risen from the dead).

## The ascension

Jesus is said to have appeared to his disciples several times before going up into heaven to be reunited with God, his Father. His rise into heaven is known as his ascension. Many Christians today believe that when they die, their soul will go to heaven to be with God and Jesus.

This stained-glass window from a church in France shows the crucifixion of Jesus. The two figures next to Jesus are traditionally Mary, his mother, and John, one of the disciples.

┌─ INTERNET LINKS ─

For links to websites where you can look into the life of Jesus, his parables and prayers, and find out more about the events surrounding his death, go to **www.usborne-quicklinks.com**

## The Bible

Christian teaching is written in the *Bible*. It is divided into two parts: the *Old* and *New Testaments*. Another word for testament is promise or covenant. The *Bible* is used by Christians during worship, study and for help during difficult times. Most importantly, Christians believe that it contains guidelines on how to live their life.

In the Middle Ages, monks used to make beautiful handwritten copies of the *Bible*. This is the beginning of one of the books in a *Bible* dating from the twelfth century.

## The Old Testament

The *Old Testament* was written in Hebrew and is almost the same as the Jewish *Tenakh* (see page 28). It tells the story of the creation of the world, the history of the Jews, and the relationship between the Jews and God. It also teaches that salvation comes through following God's law.

The *Bible* has been taken to many countries and translated into many languages. This photograph shows illustrations from a thousand-year-old Ethiopian *Bible*.

## The New Testament

The *New Testament* was written in Greek. It tells of the life of Jesus, and how, through him, God could enter into a new relationship with all people. It teaches that salvation comes through belief in the death and resurrection of Jesus. The *New Testament* is made up of 27 books: four gospels, 21 epistles, and two other books, called *Acts* and *Revelation*.

## The gospels

Gospel is a word meaning "good news". The gospels were probably written between 70 and 100CE, by four evangelists: Matthew, Mark, Luke and John. Evangelist means "announcer of good news". Each gospel tells of the life, teaching, death and resurrection of Jesus from its author's viewpoint.

Mark writing his gospel

## Acts

*Acts*, or the *Acts of the Apostles*, follows the gospels. This book continues the story after the resurrection of Jesus, and describes the early development of Christianity.

## The epistles

An epistle is a letter. Most of the epistles in the *New Testament* were written about 30 years after the death of Jesus by a converted Jew named Paul. He journeyed throughout the Roman Empire, telling non-Jews about Jesus and setting up Christian communities known as churches. Paul's letters give advice and encouragement to those early Christians.

A mosaic showing Paul

## Revelation

*Revelation* is the final book of the *New Testament*. It describes a vision of the end of time.

# Christian beliefs

Christians, like Jews, believe that the universe was created by God. According to Christian scriptures, God made the world and everything in it in six days, and on the seventh day, God rested. Some people believe that the creation story is a literal account of how the universe was created. Other people believe that it is a symbolic rather than a factual description.

*On the first day, God created day and night.*

*On the second day, God made the sky.*

*God separated the land from the seas and created vegetation on the third day.*

*On the fourth day, God created the Sun, Moon and stars.*

*God created sea creatures and birds on the fifth day.*

*Finally, on the sixth day, God created all other animals, and humans.*

Christians believe that it is wrong to act against God's laws, for example, by killing people, or stealing. Any action against God's laws is called a sin. The *Bible* teaches that Jesus, who was himself without sin, came to Earth and sacrificed his life to make possible the forgiveness of human sins.

Many Christians believe that there will be a Day of Judgement. On this day, Jesus will judge how people have behaved during their lives and decide whether their soul goes to heaven or hell.

People hold different ideas about heaven. Many believe that it is a place where people go after death to be with God. Another view is the idea of the kingdom of God on Earth, which human beings can work toward by following Christ's teaching. Hell is generally considered to be the opposite of heaven: a place of punishment, or of separation from God.

# Christian sayings

Here are some sayings associated with Christianity. These ones come mostly from the *New Testament*.

*For what shall it profit a man, if he shall gain the whole world, and lose his own soul?*

Mark's Gospel

*The truth shall make you free.*

John's Gospel

*Blessed are the peacemakers; for they shall be called the children of God.*

Matthew's Gospel (from the Sermon on the Mount)

*Do all the good you can,
By all the means you can,
In all the ways you can,
At all the times you can,
To all the people you can,
As long as ever you can.*

John Wesley

*If anyone says "I love God" and hates his brother, he is a liar; for he who does not love his brother whom he has seen, cannot love God whom he has not seen.*

John's First Letter

*And now faith, hope and love abide, these three: and the greatest of these is love.*

Paul's First Letter to the Corinthians

A cross with the body of Jesus on it reminds Christians of his crucifixion. An empty cross, like this one, is a symbol of his resurrection.

┌ INTERNET LINKS ┐
For links to websites where you can explore the Bible online, hear it read, and find out more about Christian beliefs, go to **www.usborne-quicklinks.com**

53

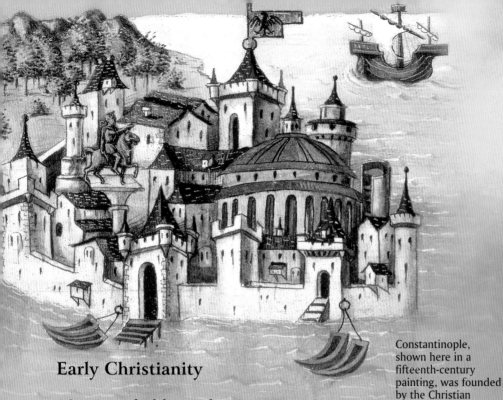

## Early Christianity

After Jesus died, his teachings were spread by his followers. Peter, one of the disciples, gave the first Christian sermon. As a result, around 3,000 people joined the new religion. Paul took the Christian message to Asia Minor (modern Turkey), Greece and even to Rome.

Some Roman emperors saw the Christians as rebels because they refused to worship Roman gods. The Roman authorities persecuted both Christians and Jews, blaming them for their own political disasters. In 70CE, the Roman army destroyed Jerusalem, hoping that this would rid the Empire of Christians and Jews alike.

To avoid arrest, Christians often had to meet in secret. They used secret signs, such as a fish, to show other Christians that it was safe to talk about their faith.

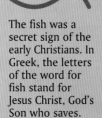

The fish was a secret sign of the early Christians. In Greek, the letters of the word for fish stand for Jesus Christ, God's Son who saves.

Constantinople, shown here in a fifteenth-century painting, was founded by the Christian Emperor Constantine.

## Constantine

In 313CE, the Roman Emperor Constantine became a Christian. He founded the city of Constantinople on the site of the old Greek city of Byzantium, and made Christianity a legal religion. In 325 he summoned a council at Nicaea (now Isnik, in Turkey) to draw up a statement of Christian belief called a creed. This became the accepted form of Christianity.

The statement, called the Nicene Creed, included the idea of the Trinity. This describes God as three persons in one: Father (the creator of all), Son (Jesus) and Holy Spirit (God's continual presence in the world). This is still a central Christian teaching.

## East and West

In the fifth and sixth centuries, the Roman Empire split in two. Constantinople was the capital of the Eastern, or Byzantine, Empire, while Rome became the capital of the Western Empire.

In 1054, there was a dispute between the head of the Church in Constantinople (the Patriarch) and the head of the Church in Rome (the Pope). This led to a major split, called the Great Schism, between the two branches of the Church.

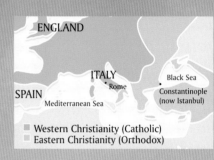

ENGLAND

ITALY
• Rome

SPAIN
Mediterranean Sea

Black Sea
Constantinople
(now Istanbul)

■ Western Christianity (Catholic)
■ Eastern Christianity (Orthodox)

The map above shows the division between Eastern and Western Christianity in 1054.

The Church in the Western Empire later became known as Roman Catholic (catholic means "universal"). The Eastern Church became known as Orthodox. Over the years, slight differences in belief and worship have grown up between the two Churches. These differences still exist today.

This mosaic shows Emperor Constantine holding a model of Constantinople, which he named after himself.

## The Reformation

By the sixteenth century, many people were unhappy with the Roman Catholic Church. A new, "reformed" type of Church, known as Protestant, grew out of the protests of people like Martin Luther and John Calvin. They criticized some of the practices of the Catholic Church which they believed had become too rich and powerful, and corrupt. This period became known as the Reformation.

## Martin Luther

In 1517, a German named Martin Luther attacked the authority of the Pope and Church leaders. He wrote a list of 95 ways in which the Catholic Church could be reformed. He was particularly opposed to the sale of indulgences. This was the Church's custom of taking money from people and in return promising that they wouldn't be punished for their sins after death.

Luther translated the *Bible* into German. Until then it had been read in Latin, which was not understood by ordinary people. It was soon translated into other languages too. Luther believed that the teachings of the *Bible* and an individual's personal faith in Christ were more important than Church rituals.

Martin Luther

## John Calvin

John Calvin, a Frenchman, gave Protestantism its organized Church structure, on which almost all later Protestant Churches were based. Calvin shared Luther's ideas but also believed in predestination: that is, the idea that God has a plan for each person, including whether or not they will be saved. Calvin's ideas became particularly popular in Switzerland and Scotland.

John Calvin, founder of the Calvinist Church

This undated woodcut was called *The troubled church in a sea of discontent*. It reflects the religious turmoil suffered during the Reformation and Counter-Reformation.

## INTERNET LINKS

For links to websites where you can find out more about early Christianity and St Paul's travels, investigate the lives of medieval monks, and learn more about Martin Luther, go to **www.usborne-quicklinks.com**

## Counter-Reformation

The Counter-Reformation was a reforming movement within the Catholic Church. In the sixteenth century, a council was formed to consider how the Church could be reformed to win people back. The Council made a number of changes, including forbidding the sale of indulgences.

Many Europeans now returned to the Catholic faith, but by and large Europe became divided into a Protestant north and a Catholic south. Catholics and Protestants hated each other, which led to intolerance, persecution and religious wars.

## The Church of England

In 1529, King Henry VIII of England challenged the supreme authority of the Pope and declared himself head of the Church in England. Under Henry's son, Edward VI, England became a Protestant country and many Catholics lost their lives. Henry's eldest daughter, Mary I, returned the country to Catholicism and during her reign many Protestants were killed.

Elizabeth I, who founded the Church of England

In 1558, Elizabeth was crowned queen. She established the Church of England: a compromise between Protestantism and Catholicism.

Today, branches of the Church of England, also known as the Anglican or Episcopalian Church, are found in many countries of the world. Branches that follow a more Catholic tradition are known as high church and those that follow a more Protestant tradition are known as low church.

Henry VIII of England

## Nonconformity

Some Protestants refused to conform to the established Churches of northern Europe and, in the seventeenth century, began to set up Nonconformist Churches. These people wanted to organize themselves. They believed that worship should be even more simple and church buildings should be even more plain.

The first Nonconformists in England were called Puritans. One of the main Puritan groups was the Quakers. You can find out more about the Quakers and several other Nonconformist groups on pages 64 to 67.

Henry VIII said that monks and nuns did not lead holy lives. He closed down the abbeys where they lived, then confiscated their wealth. Most of these abbeys are now in ruins, like Whitby Abbey, shown here.

## Voyage to America

In the seventeenth century, the threat of persecution led many Nonconformists to flee from Europe. The most famous group became known as the Pilgrim Fathers, or the Pilgrims. They were among the very first European settlers in America. They sailed from Plymouth, England, in 1620 in a ship called the *Mayflower*.

During their first winter in America, about half of the settlers died of starvation. With the help of the Native Americans, the rest survived. After their first harvest, the settlers held a feast to thank God. Thanksgiving Day is still celebrated in America every November.

## Methodism

One of the main groups to have grown out of the early Nonconformist movement is the Methodists. There are now 80 million Methodists across the world.

Methodism was founded in the eighteenth century by two English brothers, John and Charles Wesley. They preached to large, open-air congregations and won over many factory and farm workers. Methodism got its name from the methodical habits of its members, whose goal was to lead ordered, disciplined lives. They also campaigned for social reforms, such as improved education for children and more help for the poor.

John Wesley preaching

The *Mayflower II* is a replica of the ship in which a group of English Nonconformists sailed to America to avoid persecution.

## Ecumenicism

Since it began, Christianity has divided into many different branches, for example the Catholic, Orthodox and Anglican traditions. The Ecumenical movement aims to unite all Christian groups into one single, universal Church. The churches involved try to make new links between Christian movements and so bring the different branches closer together.

## Spread of faith

Since the first disciples, Christians have followed the instruction from Jesus to teach others about their faith. This means that Christianity has been spread by ordinary Christians in their everyday lives, as well as by those who have devoted their lives to converting others.

People dedicated to spreading their beliefs to people in other places are called missionaries. Christian missionaries were particularly active in Africa and Asia during the eighteenth and nineteenth centuries, and much Christian missionary work still takes place today. As well as building churches, missionaries often help to set up schools and hospitals.

David Livingstone was a Christian missionary and explorer who went to Africa in the mid nineteenth century, to spread the Christian message.

Today there are Christians in every part of the world. Just under one third of the world's population consider themselves to be Christians, and more copies of the *Bible* have been printed than any other book.

┌─ INTERNET LINKS ─────────
For links to websites where you can find out more about the Pilgrim Fathers, Methodists, missionaries and the history of the Church of England, go to **www.usborne-quicklinks.com**

## Places of worship

Christians are expected to worship together regularly, and many go to a church or chapel to do so, although worship can take place elsewhere too. Many church buildings, especially Orthodox and Catholic ones, are elaborately decorated. Protestant churches or chapels tend to be plainer. A cathedral is the principal church of a region. Churches were traditionally built in the shape of a cross, like the one below, as a reminder of Christ's crucifixion. Many Western European churches were built with the altar at the east end because this faces Jerusalem.

The picture below shows a cutaway view of an Anglican church.

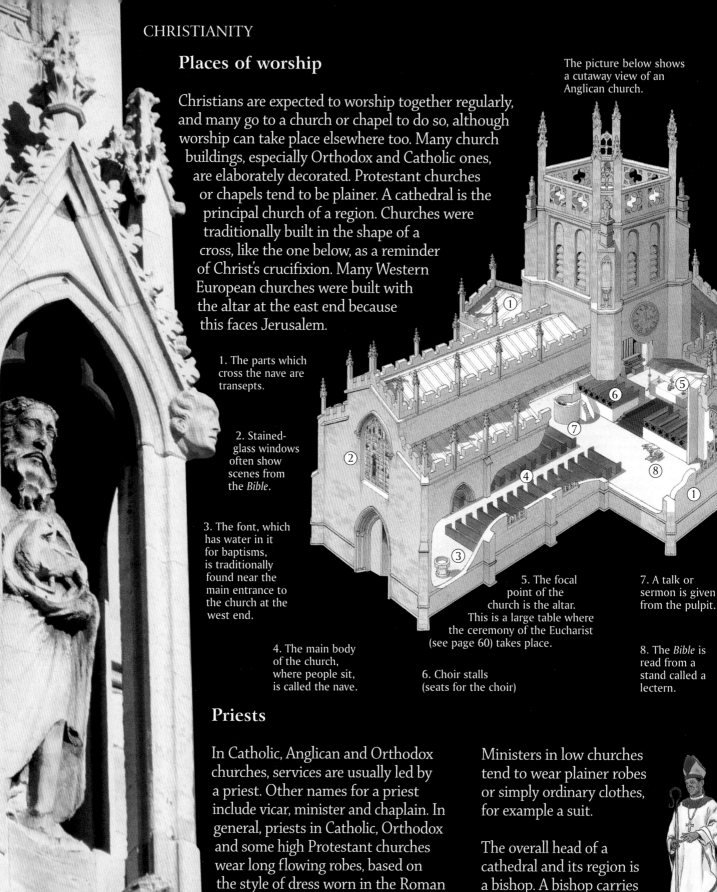

1. The parts which cross the nave are transepts.

2. Stained-glass windows often show scenes from the *Bible*.

3. The font, which has water in it for baptisms, is traditionally found near the main entrance to the church at the west end.

4. The main body of the church, where people sit, is called the nave.

5. The focal point of the church is the altar. This is a large table where the ceremony of the Eucharist (see page 60) takes place.

6. Choir stalls (seats for the choir)

7. A talk or sermon is given from the pulpit.

8. The *Bible* is read from a stand called a lectern.

## Priests

In Catholic, Anglican and Orthodox churches, services are usually led by a priest. Other names for a priest include vicar, minister and chaplain. In general, priests in Catholic, Orthodox and some high Protestant churches wear long flowing robes, based on the style of dress worn in the Roman Empire, where Christianity began.

The decorations on many churches often show people and stories from the *Bible*. The sculpture of St. John the Baptist on the left is from York Minster, in the north of England.

Ministers in low churches tend to wear plainer robes or simply ordinary clothes, for example a suit.

The overall head of a cathedral and its region is a bishop. A bishop carries a crosier, which is like a shepherd's crook. It is a reminder of his duty to look after his flock: the people in his region.

A bishop with his crosier

## Christian worship

Christian worship involves hearing readings from the *Bible*, listening to sermons (religious talks) and praising God, or asking for his help, in prayers, hymns or chants. The main act of church worship is held on a Sunday.

A sermon, also called a homily or address, is often given by a priest and is normally based on a passage from the *Bible*. In some churches, the sermon may be given from a raised platform called a pulpit (from the Latin for "platform"). Pulpits were designed so that preachers could be seen and heard.

People gathered together for worship are known as a congregation. Below you can see a congregation in the nave of Durham Cathedral, which was built in the north of England in the twelfth century.

Prayer is the way in which Christians talk to God, and prayers can be spoken aloud, or silent. Christians are encouraged to pray both with other people and on their own. A prayer can be anything a Christian wants to say to God, but often prayers are used to praise or thank God, or to ask for his help or forgiveness.

Hymns are sacred songs that praise or worship God. They were originally sung in Greek or Latin but since the Reformation (see page 55) they are mostly sung in the language of the area, for example French in France. Hymns are an important part of worship in many churches.

## Monks and nuns

Monks and nuns are men and women who have taken solemn vows dedicating their entire lives to God. They carry out this work usually by teaching, nursing or through prayer. They live together in communities called monasteries and convents. The vows people make to become Christian monks or nuns include giving up all their possessions, leaving their friends and family, and being obedient to the head of their monastery or convent.

### INTERNET LINKS

For links to websites where you can explore church buildings online, learn more about Christian clergy, monks and nuns, and listen to Christian music, go to **www.usborne-quicklinks.com**

## The Eucharist

The main service in many churches is the Eucharist, which means "thanksgiving". It is a re-enactment of the Last Supper (see page 51) in which Christians eat a small piece of bread or a wafer, and sip a drop of wine.

Bread and wine

For many Christians, the bread or wafer represents the body of Jesus Christ. The wine represents his blood. Together they remind Christians that Jesus gave his life so that people could enter a new, closer relationship with God.

The most holy part of the Eucharist is when the priest blesses the bread. Here, a Russian Orthodox archbishop is holding up a Russian Orthodox three-bar cross as he blesses the bread during a Mass.

This service has a slightly different significance for different branches of the Church and they call it by different names. It is usually called Mass in Catholic churches, Holy Communion in some Anglican churches and the Divine Liturgy in Orthodox churches. Protestants often call it the Breaking of Bread or the Lord's Supper.

## Baptism

People are welcomed into the Christian faith by a baptism ceremony (see page 49). In some branches of Christianity, baptism involves people having a little water poured on their head instead of being totally immersed. Some branches of Christianity only baptize adult believers but most baptize children, usually as babies.

In some churches, baptisms take place in a font like this.

The parents choose close friends or relations to be godparents to the child. At the baptism ceremony, both the parents and godparents promise to bring the child up as a Christian. At an infant baptism the baby is also officially given its Christian (first) names. This is why a baptism is sometimes referred to as a christening.

## Confirmation

At a confirmation ceremony, a person becomes a full adult member of their church. They take on the promises that were made on their behalf at baptism.

A confirmation ceremony

During the ceremony the local bishop lays his hands on the person's head to "confirm" the help of the Holy Spirit in living a Christian life. The age at which people are confirmed varies from church to church.

## Marriage

Christian marriages usually take place in a church. Before a couple can be married many churches require the couple's banns to be read. This means that the details of their marriage have to be announced in church. This ritual dates back to medieval times and was intended to prevent people who were closely related from marrying and also anyone who had already promised to marry someone else.

In the ceremony itself, a priest, acting as God's representative, joins together the couple as husband and wife. The bride and groom make solemn vows to love and look after each other. Christians believe that the vows are sacred because they are made in the presence of God, as well as family and friends. Prayers are usually said and there may be readings from the *Bible*.

Christian marriage is intended to be a lifelong commitment. This intent is symbolized by the giving and receiving of a ring or rings. In some services, after the exchange of vows and rings, the couple share bread and wine (see "The Eucharist", opposite).

Christian weddings usually take place in a church and are conducted by an ordained priest. Family and friends gather to witness the ceremony.

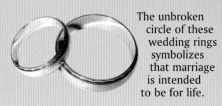

The unbroken circle of these wedding rings symbolizes that marriage is intended to be for life.

## Ordination

Ordination is a ceremony at which a person becomes a priest or equivalent, depending on the type of Church. It also takes place in some Churches when a priest is promoted to a higher post, such as that of bishop.

A *Bible* may be given as an ordination gift.

During the ordination, the minister performing the ceremony may lay his hands on the head of the person being ordained. This has been adapted from a Jewish custom for ordaining rabbis (teachers of the faith) by the laying on of hands.

## Holy unction

Holy unction, or extreme unction in the Catholic Church, is the smearing of holy oil onto a sick or dying person by a priest.

It is accompanied by prayers and words of comfort, and is used to give spiritual help and sometimes to encourage the physical healing of the sick person.

## Death customs

What happens to a person's body after death may depend on a particular belief about the afterlife.

Orthodox Christians, for example, will bury bodies but not cremate them. They believe that the body has to be kept in one piece so that it can come back to life on the Day of Judgement (see page 53).

Other Christians believe that having the body cremated does not stop the soul from coming back to be judged. They leave the choice of cremation or burial to the individual and the family.

INTERNET LINKS

For links to websites where you can discover more about Christian ceremonies, including Baptism and Communion, go to
**www.usborne-quicklinks.com**

# Christian festivals

There are a number of Christian festivals celebrated during the year. These are mostly based on events that occurred during the life of Jesus, for example, Christmas and Easter. The Western and Orthodox Churches use different calendars, so they celebrate these festivals at different times.

## Advent

Advent begins with the fourth Sunday before Christmas and it marks the start of the Christian Church's year. Advent means "coming" or "drawing near". Christians use this period to prepare themselves for Christmas, the celebration of the anniversary of the birth of Jesus in Bethlehem.

In many churches and chapels one candle is lit on each of the four Sundays during Advent. Children may also have an Advent calendar or candle to count down the days from the beginning of December to Christmas Day.

Advent candles

## Christmas

Christmas, which means "Christ's Mass", is the celebration of the birth of Jesus. Although the exact date of his birth is not known, the celebration is held in the West on December 25th.

Christmas Mass being celebrated at a church in Alsace, France. The figure of Christ on the cross hangs above the congregation.

This date was probably chosen because, as a great prophet, Jesus was believed to have both been conceived and to have died on the same day of the year – in his case, March 25th (Passover) – and then born exactly nine months later. In the Orthodox Church, which uses a different calendar, Christmas is on January 7th.

In church at Christmas, the story of the birth of Jesus is read, and carols (hymns about the story of his birth) are sung. There may be symbols of the birth story on display, such as figures of the holy family, shepherds and angels.

# Lent

Lent is the period before Easter when Christians remember their sins. It used to be a time of fasting (not eating) but today people are more likely to try to give up a particular thing they enjoy. Lent commemorates the 40 days and nights that Jesus spent fasting and praying in the wilderness.

The day before Lent starts is called Shrove Tuesday, Mardi Gras or Pancake Day. This is a time of celebration before Lent begins. In many countries there are parades with costumes, singing and dancing. In some countries people make pancakes. This was traditionally done as a way of using up food before the fasting period began.

On the first day of Lent, which is called Ash Wednesday, some Christians mark their foreheads with ash. This is a sign that they are humble before God. It is also a symbol of the sorrow and mourning caused by sin.

The ash used on Ash Wednesday is often made from burned palm crosses like this, saved from Palm Sunday of the previous year.

On the Sunday before Easter, called Palm Sunday, Many Christians are given a cross made from palm leaves. This is in memory of the entry of Jesus into Jerusalem, when the crowds waved palm leaves to welcome him.

## Holy Week and Easter

Palm Sunday marks the beginning of Holy Week. During this week, Christians remember the events from the arrival of Jesus in Jerusalem to the day of his resurrection, Easter Day. The day when people remember the death of Jesus is called Good Friday. This is because Christians believe that allowing himself to be crucified was an act of supreme goodness for all.

Easter is the most important Christian festival, and special church services are held. It coincides with, and gets its name from, an earlier, pre-Christian spring festival.

This man is taking part in a Holy Week procession in Seville, Spain. He belongs to a Roman Catholic Guild whose members pray and fast on behalf of the whole community. The medieval-style hood hides the face, as the *Bible* says a person should not make a show of fasting or praying.

## Other festivals

Christians hold special church or chapel services to celebrate other important events. These include Ascension Day, which reminds Christians of the ascension of Jesus into heaven, and Pentecost (also called Whitsun), which is seven Sundays after Easter.

Pentecost marks the day, fifty days after the resurrection, when God's Holy Spirit is said to have come to the disciples in the form of wind and fire. All Christians were traditionally baptized at Pentecost and the term Whitsun, or White Sunday, comes from the white robes worn by new Christians as a sign of their purity.

## The mother of Jesus

All Christians respect Mary as the mother of Jesus, chosen by God, but the Catholic and Orthodox Churches give her a special role. They believe that if they pray to Mary she will plead with Jesus on their behalf. They hold special services to celebrate events in her life, such as the Annunciation: when the angel told her that she would be the mother of Jesus.

In many Catholic and Orthodox churches, statues of the Virgin Mary are decorated with flowers on festival days during which events in her life are celebrated.

## Saints' days

Saints are people who are officially recognized by the Catholic and Orthodox Churches as having lived particularly holy lives. There are special days of remembrance for many saints, usually on the date of their death. On these days there may be processions and special church services.

INTERNET LINKS

For links to websites where you can find out more about Christian festivals, and read stories about Christian saints, go to
**www.usborne-quicklinks.com**

# NONCONFORMISTS

✝ Most of the groups listed on these pages grew out of the Protestant, Nonconformist movement in Christianity (see page 56). Some have tens of millions of members. A few of the groups do not regard themselves as Christians and a few are not considered to be Christians by other groups. They are arranged alphabetically.

The plain design of this Lutheran church in Iceland reflects the uncluttered style of Lutheran worship.

## Baptists

The first Baptist Church in Britain dates from the early seventeenth century. Believers broke away from the Church of England because they felt that the head of their Church was Jesus, not a king or queen. Baptists are now one of the largest Protestant groups, with over 41 million members worldwide.

As in most Baptist baptisms, this woman is lain backward in the water in the position of a person in a coffin, as a symbol that she is leaving behind her old life. Like Jesus, she'll symbolically rise from death to a new life.

Baptists stress the importance of the teachings of the *Bible* as well as personal faith in Jesus. They baptize only people who have a personal faith, so do not baptize babies and children who are too young to understand the significance of the ceremony. This is called Believers' Baptism and, in a Baptist church, involves full immersion in the water.

## Christian Scientists

Christian Science was discovered in 1866 in America by Mary Baker Eddy. In 1879, she founded a church designed to share the message of God's power to heal people, as shown by Jesus. Her book, *Science and Health with Key to the Scriptures*, teaches that God's laws can be understood and used, bringing healing to any situation or condition.

*Heal the sick, cleanse the lepers, raise the dead, cast out demons. Freely you have received, freely give.*
New Testament (Matthew's Gospel)

## Church of Christ

Members of the Churches of Christ are found in over 170 countries, with the largest number of congregations in the USA, Africa and India. They follow strictly the teachings of the *New Testament* (see page 52) and reject all other traditions and creeds.

## Congregationalists

Each Congregational church is independent and governs itself. This means that the beliefs of Congregationalists can vary from one church to another. Beliefs also vary among individuals as each person shapes their own faith and develops their own direct relationship with God. The movement began in the sixteenth century. It is popular in the USA, Eastern Europe and Britain.

## Holiness Movement

There are many different types of Churches in the Holiness Movement but all are dedicated to striving for holy living by following the teachings of Jesus. This movement rejects the materialistic values of modern society and stresses the importance of the spiritual life. The largest Holiness Church is the Church of the Nazarene.

*Be perfect ... as your heavenly Father is perfect.*
New Testament (Matthew's Gospel)

## The second coming

This is described in the Bible as the time when Christ will come again. Then, the Day of Judgement will take place: both the living and the dead will be judged on their deeds and their faith, and God's kingdom will be established here on Earth. Some Christians believe that at the second coming, people will be sent either to heaven or hell after being judged. Many believe that God's kingdom will be for all Christians or even for all humanity.

## Jehovah's Witnesses

The modern history of Jehovah's Witnesses started in America in the 1870s. Charles Taze Russell played a key role. Jehovah is the name for God in the *Old Testament* (see page 52).

Jehovah's Witnesses believe that very soon Jesus will replace human rule and reign for a thousand years, with millions of people being saved. Witnesses feel that it is their Christian duty to preach this good news from house to house.

Witnesses live by the strict moral code of the *Bible*. They do not believe in the Trinity (see page 54) and believe that theirs is the true religion. They meet in halls known as Kingdom Halls.

*This gospel of the kingdom will be preached in the whole world as a testimony to all nations, and then the end will come.*
New Testament (Matthew's Gospel)

## Lutherans

The Lutheran Church is based on the ideas of Martin Luther (see page 55). With many members worldwide, it is one of the most important denominations in Germany (with Roman Catholicism) and the dominant church in most Scandinavian countries. Lutherans are committed to the search for unity among all Christian groups and see the protection of human rights as an important Christian concern.

**INTERNET LINKS**

For links to websites where you can learn more about the beliefs of Baptists and other nonconformist groups, go to **www.usborne-quicklinks.com**

## Mennonites

A movement which originated in the sixteenth-century Reformation (see page 55), Mennonites derive their name from Menno Simons of the Netherlands. Today they have about 1.7 million members worldwide. They are similar to Baptists, follow Jesus and emphasize non-violence.

## Methodists

You can find out more about Methodists on page 57.

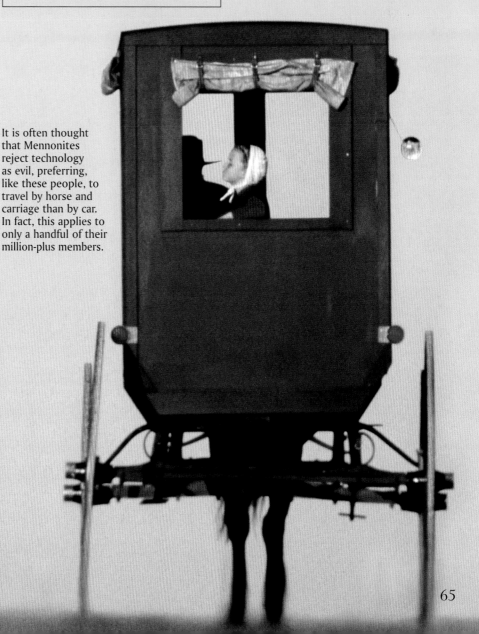

It is often thought that Mennonites reject technology as evil, preferring, like these people, to travel by horse and carriage than by car. In fact, this applies to only a handful of their million-plus members.

# Latter-day Saints ("Mormons")

The Church of Jesus Christ of Latter-day Saints was founded in America in 1830, when Joseph Smith published the *Book of Mormon: Another Testament of Jesus Christ*. This is believed to be a religious account of ancient American civilizations and suggests that America will be one of the two places (the other one being Jerusalem) from which Christ will rule when he comes again. Church members view it as a companion scripture to the *Bible* and once gained the nickname "Mormons" from it.

The organization of the Church is based on that of the original Christian Church (see page 54). There are twelve men who have been chosen to be present-day apostles (disciples). The President of the Church is regarded as a prophet, who continues to reveal truths from God. As appropriate, these are added to their official list of recognized scriptures.

The Church only baptizes children of eight and over, who are thought of as old enough to be accountable for their actions. Church members can be baptized on behalf of their dead ancestors. They believe that marriage is very important and that if it takes place in a temple, it can last for eternity.

Marriages, baptisms and other special ceremonies of Latter-day Saints take place in temples, like this one at La Jolla in California, USA. For ordinary worship, people go to their local chapel. Many temples are finished in white stone. White is often associated with purity.

# Pentecostalists

The Pentecostal Movement began in America at the beginning of the twentieth century and is now one of the fastest-growing branches of Christianity. Its members attach great importance to the Day of Pentecost (see page 63) and the work of the Holy Spirit. They believe the Holy Spirit gave the disciples the ability to "speak in tongues", that is, in languages other than their own.

The Holy Spirit and the disciples at Pentecost

Pentecostal worship is emotional and spontaneous depending on how the Holy Spirit moves each individual. Pentecostalists often "speak in tongues" and tell of life-changing personal experiences. They believe in faith healing: the healing of illness through the power of people's faith in the Holy Spirit. The Pentecostalist style of worship has influenced many different types of Churches. Pentecostalists are sometimes known as Charismatics.

*All of them were filled with the Holy Spirit and began to speak in other tongues as the Spirit enabled them.*
New Testament (Acts)

# Presbyterians

Presbyterianism is based on the ideas of John Calvin (see page 55). It is one of the Protestant family of Churches and is found especially in the Netherlands, Scotland, the USA and Korea. The Church of Scotland is Presbyterian.

## Quakers

The proper name for Quakers is the Religious Society of Friends. The Society was founded in the seventeenth century in England by George Fox. The nickname, Quakers, came from a speech made by Fox, in which he said, "You should quake at the word of the Lord."

One of the main Quaker beliefs is that each person has a direct relationship with God, so they don't have priests or rituals. Worship, which is held in Meeting Houses, is mainly silent until someone feels moved by the Holy Spirit to speak. Quakers refer to their sense of God in their soul as "inner light". The Society is known for its pacifism and charity work.

*For you are all the children of light and children of the day.*
New Testament (Thessalonians)

## Salvation Army

The Salvation Army, a branch of the Christian Church, is at work in 126 countries worldwide. It was founded in 1865 by William Booth, who believed that he was called to fight poverty and social injustice by meeting both people's physical and spiritual needs. The Salvation Army's social work includes shelters for the homeless, elderly care homes, schools, hospitals, support for communities and families, and services for people with drug and alcohol addictions.

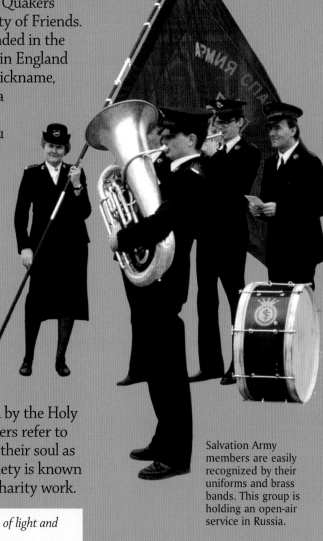

Salvation Army members are easily recognized by their uniforms and brass bands. This group is holding an open-air service in Russia.

## Seventh-day Adventists

An Adventist believes that Christ's second coming (see page 65) is very close. Seventh-day Adventists worship on the Sabbath: from sunset on Friday to sunset on Saturday. They live by the teachings of the *Bible* and are also guided by the writings of Ellen White, one of the founders of the movement. The Seventh-day Adventist church was formally established in the USA in 1863. Since then it has grown and now has over 18 million members worldwide.

## Unitarians

Unitarians emphasize reason, tolerance, human rights and understanding between faiths. Some see themselves as Christians, some do not. They find the oneness of God more believable than the idea of the Trinity (see page 54) and see Jesus as human.

*We ask all alike to think, not all to think alike.*
Unitarian Church

## United Reformed Church

The United Reformed Church was formed in Britain in 1972. It brings together members from three of the Reformed traditions which grew out of the Reformation (see page 55), namely Presbyterians, Congregationalists and Churches of Christ.

## Evangelicals

This term usually refers to Protestants who converted to Christianity after an intense experience. "Evangelical" has the same root as "evangelist", which means "announcer of good news". Evangelicals are enthusiastic in their efforts to convert others. They stress the importance of the *Bible* and personal faith in Jesus rather than Church rituals.

INTERNET LINKS
For links to websites where you can learn more about the beliefs of Latter-day Saints and other nonconformist groups, go to **www.usborne-quicklinks.com**

# ISLAM

Islam means obedience to the will of Allah (God). Followers of Islam are called Muslims, which means "obedient ones". Muslims believe that God's word was revealed to a man called Muhammad in the early seventh century CE. Muhammad became known as the Messenger of God, or the Prophet. There are about 1.6 billion Muslims in the world today, mainly in the Middle East, North Africa and parts of Asia.

This Muslim boy is reading the *Qur'an*. Muslims believe that the book contains the word of God as revealed to Muhammad.

## Muhammad's early life

Muhammad was born in Makkah, in what is now Saudi Arabia, in about 570CE. Brought up by a generous uncle, he became a camel-driver, trader, husband and father. He was respected in the community and was known as the Trusted One.

Muhammad's life was not completely happy, though. He disapproved of the lawlessness of his fellow people and was troubled by their belief in many gods. The belief in one God, as upheld by Abraham (see page 25), had previously spread to Arabia but had since been all but lost.

## God speaks

Muhammad used to go into the mountains to pray and think. Around his fortieth birthday, while he was in a cave on Mount Nur, near Makkah, God spoke to him for the first time through the angel Jibril (Gabriel). Jibril said that Muhammad must tell the people of Makkah to turn away from their gods, and worship Allah, the one true god. (Allah is the Arabic word for God.)

Throughout the rest of his life, Muhammad continued to receive messages from God through Jibril. They were later written down as the Muslim holy books.

This sixteenth-century Persian painting shows Muhammad being visited by holy men and an angel. The Prophet's face is hidden, in accordance with Islamic artistic tradition.

## The migration

Muhammad began to preach in Makkah. His central message was that "there is no god but Allah". His followers grew in number and, fearing Muhammad's popularity and power, the political leaders began to plot against him. In 622, Muhammad and his followers fled to the city now called Madinah, City of the Prophet. The story below tells how Allah helped Muhammad on his journey.

*Muhammad and his friend, Abu Bakr, were hiding in a cave when they heard soldiers coming. Muhammad told his fearful friend that Allah would save them.*

*One soldier approached the cave but stopped. A huge spider's web stretched across the mouth of the cave.*

*"No point going in there," he shouted to his men. "No-one could have got in without breaking that web."*

*With that, the soldiers shrugged their shoulders and marched away. And so Muhammad was saved.*

— Mediterranean Sea

•Madinah
•Makkah
ARABIA
Red Sea
AFRICA
• Important places in the life of Muhammad

The journey to Madinah is known as the *Hijrah*, or migration. It is such an important event that Muslims date their calendar from it. According to the Islamic calendar it is now the fifteenth century. In Madinah, Muhammad's following grew very strong. In 629, the Muslims were able to conquer Makkah, and Muhammad was finally accepted there as the Prophet of God. He won respect both as a religious leader and as a statesman.

## Muhammad's death

After the death of Muhammad in 632, Abu Bakr made an announcement to those who could not believe that he had really died. He said, "Those of you who worship Muhammad must accept that Muhammad is dead. As for those of you who worship Allah, Allah is living and will never die."

This shows the Muslim attitude to Muhammad. Muslims do not worship Muhammad but, as Allah's messenger, he is regarded with the greatest respect. For this reason, whenever Muslims say or write Muhammad's name, they also add the words "Peace be upon him".

┌─INTERNET LINKS─
For links to websites about Islam, and the life of the prophet Muhammad, go to **www.usborne-quicklinks.com**

## Islamic sayings

Below are a few sayings from Islam. Underneath them are the names of the people who said them or the scriptures from which they are taken.

*In the whole universe of creation there is nothing that is either the like or the equal or the contrary of God. God is Exalted above all form, indeed immune to and free from form.*

Ibrahim Haqqi

*Whatever good happens to you is from God: and whatever evil happens to you is from yourself.*

Qur'an

*Three things cannot be retrieved:
The arrow once sped from the bow.
The word spoken in haste,
The missed opportunity.*

Ali, Caliph of Islam

*The best Islam consists in feeding the hungry and in greeting those one knows and those one does not know, too.*

Muhammad

*Trust in God – but tie your camel first.*

Muhammad

*Not one of you is a believer until he loves for his brother what he loves for himself.*

Muhammad

*What actions are most excellent? To gladden the heart of human beings, to feed the hungry, to help the afflicted, to lighten the sorrow of the sorrowful, and to remove the sufferings of the injured.*

Muhammad

*I believe in Allah, His Angels, His Books, His Messengers, the Last Day, and that everything good or bad is decided by Allah the Almighty, and in the life after death.*

A statement of Islamic belief

## Sacred writings

The *Qur'an* is the Islamic holy book. It is believed to be the word of Allah revealed to Muhammad during the last 22 years of his life, so Allah, not Muhammad, is the author. At first the revelations were memorized and passed on by word of mouth, but it wasn't long before they were written down. The writings were not collected into one book until after the prophet's death.

The *Qur'an* is written in Arabic script. Some pages are richly decorated with floral patterns.

As the *Qur'an* is seen as the word of Allah, most Muslims try to learn to read it in its original Arabic, even if this is not their own language. They read part of it every day and usually wash as a sign of respect before touching it.

The collective name for Muhammad's words and deeds is the *Sunnah*. These were recorded in writings called *Hadiths*, which help to interpret the *Qur'an*. They give further guidance on worship, belief and how to behave.

This girl is following the *Qur'an's* teaching which says that a Muslim should pray five times a day.

## Muslim beliefs

There are seven main Islamic beliefs. Muslims believe in Allah, the true God; angels; the holy books; the prophets (see below); the Day of Judgement; life after death and the idea that God controls all that happens.

The beliefs of Islam can be written in Arabic calligraphy like this to form the shape of a boat. Muslims call it the Ship of Life.

## The prophets and books

Muslims believe in the prophets of the *Tenakh* and *Bible*, such as Adam, Ibrahim (Abraham), Musa (Moses) and Dawud (David). Muslims respect Isa (Jesus) as an important prophet though, unlike Christians, they do not see him as the son of God. They regard Muhammad as the last of the prophets, who received the final and perfect message from God.

Islam teaches that many of these prophets were also given messages from God. Although these messages were written down, Muslims believe that they no longer exist in their original form. Muslims call Jews and Christians "People of the Book" out of respect for their belief in the *Tenakh* and *Bible*.

She has positioned her prayer mat so that it faces in the direction of the *Ka'bah* in Makkah.

## The Day of Judgement

After death, Muslims believe that the deeds of every person will be weighed. People whose good deeds outweigh their bad deeds will be able to cross a narrow pathway across hellfire and safely reach Paradise. This will take place on the Day of Judgement.

## The will of Allah

The *Qur'an* teaches that God is in control of everything that happens. This is linked to the idea of obedience, and Muslims try to do the will of Allah rather than following an individual path through life.

## The Five Pillars of Islam

The Five Pillars of Islam show how Islamic beliefs should be put into action in daily life.

1. The *Shahadah*
This is the declaration of faith, which is repeated several times a day: "There is no God but Allah, and Muhammad is His messenger."

2. *Salah*
These are the five daily prayers which are said, in Arabic, at dawn, just after midday, mid-afternoon, just after sunset and after dark. The prayers may be said in any clean place, and extra prayers may be offered at any time. They consist mainly of verses from the *Qur'an*, praising Allah and asking for guidance.

3. *Zakah*
This is the duty, for Muslims who can afford it, to give at least 2.5% of their savings and other valuables every year to the poor.

This painting from the side of a house shows a pilgrim's experience of the *Hajj*. The black box in the middle is the *Ka'bah*. Surrounding it is a crowd of pilgrims.

4. *Sawm*
This means fasting. During the ninth Islamic month, *Ramadan*, Muslims eat and drink nothing during daylight hours. The reason given by Allah in the *Qur'an* is that this helps people to become more aware of Allah. *Ramadan* is a time for studying the *Qur'an*, showing self-control, and caring for others.

5. *Hajj*
This is a pilgrimage to Makkah which involves visiting the *Ka'bah*. This is a place of worship that is thought to have been built by Ibrahim and one of his sons, Isma'il.

The *Ka'bah* had fallen into misuse but Muhammad restored it to the worship of Allah. The *Hajj* takes place during the twelfth Islamic month. Nobody is allowed to go on *Hajj* without making sure that their family is provided for while they are away. The poor, old and sick do not have to go. Men wear white garments to enter Makkah at *Hajj*, as a sign that all are equal.

┌INTERNET LINKS┐
For links to websites where you can learn more about Islamic beliefs, the *Hajj* and the *Qur'an*, go to
**www.usborne-quicklinks.com**

# The spread of Islam

After Muhammad's death, the Muslims were ruled by a series of leaders called *caliphs* (*caliph* means "successor"). The first of these was Muhammad's friend, Abu Bakr.

The *caliphs* waged many wars with the intention both of defending Islam and spreading it. People in conquered countries were supposed to be allowed to keep their religion but had to pay extra taxes, as they were excused from *zakah* (see page 71) and from military service.

In 661, the Islamic capital moved from Makkah to Damascus in Syria. In 750, it moved again, to Baghdad in Iraq, where it was to remain for the next 500 years.

In the eighth century, the Muslims conquered much of Spain and Portugal. They ruled there right up until the late fifteenth century, when the Christians of Spain and Portugal joined forces to overthrow them.

SPAIN

Mediterranean Sea

NORTH AFRICA

Damascus

• Baghdad

• Makkah

ARABIA

Arabian Sea

☐ Spread of Islam during Muhammad's lifetime
☐ Area conquered under the first four *caliphs* (632-661)
☐ Area conquered between 661 and 750

The map above shows how far Islam spread in just over 100 years following Muhammad's death.

## Muslim scholarship

As well as spreading the Islamic faith, Muslims played a large part in the development and spread of learning. Mathematics and science, including medicine and astronomy, as well as art, all flourished in the Muslim world, especially between about 900 and 1200.

Muslim architects designed innovative two-tiered arches to raise the roof of their Great Mosque at Cordoba in Spain.

As early as the tenth century, the Spanish town of Cordoba had no fewer than 70 libraries. In Baghdad a "house of wisdom" was built. This was a great library in which the *caliph* wanted to collect copies of all the books in the world.

It was Muslim scholars who introduced many of the works and ideas from the Ancient Greeks and Persians to Europeans. They replaced the clumsy Roman numeral system with Arabic numerals. They also adopted and established the decimal system of writing numbers in tens, hundreds, thousands and so on, as well as the concept of zero from India.

A perpetual-motion machine like this was described in a book on waterwheels in the heyday of Muslim scholarship.

Arabic numeral 7 and the Roman numerals used previously.

$$7 = VII$$

The domes and minarets (towers) on this Istanbul skyline are typical features of Islamic architecture.

# Later Islamic empires

In the sixteenth and seventeenth centuries, three powerful Islamic empires were at their height. They were renowned for the magnificence of their rulers' courts. The Ottoman Empire lasted the longest, from the fourteenth century until 1923. It first spread out from what is now Turkey. By the end of the fifteenth century, Muslims had conquered most of the Christian Byzantine world including Constantinople, which they renamed Istanbul.

The map above shows the extent of the three Islamic empires.

## Sunni and Shia Islam

There are two main branches in Islam: Sunni and Shia Islam. They formed shortly after Muhammad's death, when his followers argued over who should lead them. One group, later to become the Sunnis, saw Abu Bakr as Muhammad's rightful successor. Another, which became the Shiites, saw the fourth *caliph*, Muhammad's cousin and son-in-law, Ali, as his first true heir.

About 87% of the world's Muslims are Sunnis. Sunni means "the path shown by Muhammad". Shia Islam is dominant in Iran, and in Iraq there are more Shiites than Sunnis. Bahrain, Lebanon, Azerbaijan, Yemen, Turkey and Pakistan also have significant numbers of Shiites.

Shiites and Sunnis share views on the *Qur'an*, Muhammad, God and worship, but differ slightly in the ways they put the teachings of Islam into practice. Also, Shiite Muslims put particular emphasis on the virtue of suffering for their faith. They regard as a martyr Ali's son Hussein, who was murdered in a political struggle.

The building on the left is the Sultanahmet Mosque, a Muslim place of worship which was built in the seventeenth century.

# Sufism

A small number of Muslims, known as Sufis, seek to find a close personal relationship with God and gain inner knowledge directly from him. This approach to Islam, called Sufism, emerged from about 800CE. Sufis come from both the Sunni and Shia traditions, although some Sunni Muslims don't think that Sufism is an acceptable Islamic practice. Sufi worship includes music, chanting, dancing and meditation. These are believed to help Sufis to achieve a state in which they can be closer to God.

Some members of a small group of Sufis in Turkey have become famous for a ritual dance called the *sema* in which they twirl around energetically. The dancers are known as whirling dervishes. Dervish means "wandering beggar"; the first Sufis were wandering holy men who lived without possessions.

—INTERNET LINKS—

For links to websites where you can discover more about the history of Islam, and Muslim scientists and thinkers, go to **www.usborne-quicklinks.com**

73

## Places of worship

Muslims go to mosques to pray together and meet other Muslims. The Arabic for mosque is *masjid*, meaning "place of prostration". As well as a main prayer room, there are rooms for studying, and for teaching children. Outside the mosque there may be a courtyard with places for ritual washing.

Some mosques may have a crescent and star on them. These have no real religious significance but came to be associated with Islam because of its lunar calendar and because the *Qur'an* speaks of stars as being one of Allah's signs.

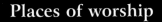

Star and crescent

The Jumeira Mosque in Dubai, United Arab Emirates has features that are common to most mosques. The tall, ornate towers are minarets. The call to prayer goes out from here.

Almost all mosques have at least one tower, called a minaret. At five set times each day, the mosque relays the Arabic call to prayer, often by loudspeaker, from a minaret. This call to prayer is called the *Adhan*, and the person who recites it is called the *mu'adhin*.

### The Adhan

*Allah is the greatest.*
*I bear witness that there is no God but Allah.*
*I bear witness that Muhammad is the messenger of God.*
*Hurry to prayer:*
*Hurry to success:*
*Allah is the greatest.*

The main part of the mosque is a large, rectangular prayer hall. Its walls may be plain, or decorated with painted patterns, or tiles: there are no pictures or statues.

The central domed roof was originally designed to keep the prayer hall below cool, especially in hot countries. Later, domes became more of a traditional feature of mosque architecture.

The wall that faces Makk[ah] has a small niche in it ca[lled] a *mihrab*. This draws peo[ple's] attention in the directio[n of] the *Ka'bah* (see page 71).

To the right of the *mihra[b]* [is a] raised platform, or *minba[r]* usually has three steps. I[n the] early days of Islam, Muha[mmad] preached to his follower[s from] the top step of the *min[bar]* leaving the platform its[elf] empty as a sign of resp[ect to] Allah. Talks in the mos[que are] given from the middle s[tep] below Muhammad. In s[ome] countries there is a read[er] to the left of the *mihra[b]* [where the] *Qur'an* is read from.

Key to floorplan

↑ To Makka[h]

**1** Mihrab    **3** Mi[naret]
**2** Minbar    **4** W[ashing area]

Dome

Floorplan of a typical mosque

Smaller decorative domes cover other areas of the mosque.

74

## Worship

All male Muslims are expected to attend the mosque on Fridays for prayers at noon. Women who go to the mosque usually sit separately in a screened-off area. Women must cover their heads for prayer. Men don't have to, although many choose to.

Before entering the mosque, Muslims must wash their hands, arms, face and feet, to prepare for prayer and as a sign of respect for Allah. This ritual washing is called *wudu*. Muslims also take off their shoes before praying, as the place where they pray must be clean. There are no seats in the prayer hall, so people sit or kneel on the floor. When praying other than at the mosque, Muslims kneel on a prayer mat for cleanliness.

*Muslims use prayer mats so that the place where they pray is always spotlessly clean.*

Muslims always pray facing the direction of the *Ka'bah* in Makkah. In the mosque, this is shown by the *mihrab*. Some modern prayer mats have a built-in compass pointing to Makkah.

Worship in the mosque is led by an *imam*, or "man of knowledge". The prayers are said in Arabic, and are accompanied by movements called *rakahs*. They are believed to have been taught by Muhammad himself.

Each *rakah* involves the whole body, as a sign of being totally humble before God. The *imam* performs the *rakahs*, copied by the people. Some of the main *rakahs* are described below.

*Standing upright, raise the hands level to the shoulders, with the fingers apart.*

*Bow from the waist keeping the back and head level, with the hands resting on the knees.*

*Kneel with the hands flat on the floor and the nose and forehead touching the ground.*

Some Muslims use beads to help them concentrate as they pray. A person holds each bead in turn, while reciting one of the 99 names of Allah, known as the "Most Beautiful Names".

There are 99 beads on this string, one for each name of Allah. The gold beads mark places where a Muslim stops reciting the names and says a prayer.

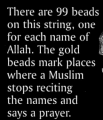

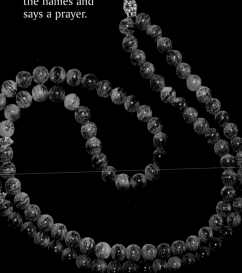

## Islamic art

The *Qur'an* forbids images of any kind to be made of Allah or Muhammad, or indeed of any person or animal. This is partly because the worship of images is forbidden in Islam, and partly because Muslims believe that no artistic representation could ever be good enough to reflect the magnificence of Allah's creation.

Islamic artists have therefore concentrated on designing geometric patterns. The art of writing, or calligraphy, is also important. Muslim calligraphers create beautiful pictures, using texts from the *Qur'an*, prayers, and the names of God.

Part of a mosaic wall in the nineteenth-century Kazimayn Mosque in Baghdad, Iraq

┌INTERNET LINKS─────
For links to websites where you can find out more about mosques and Islamic forms of worship, go to **www.usborne-quicklinks.com**

75

## Islam in everyday life

The religious laws of Islam come from the *Qur'an* and the *Sunnah*, and are called the *Shari'ah*, which means the "clear, straight path". They are guidelines on matters ranging from a person's actions to affairs of state. In Muslim countries, such as Iran, there is little difference between religious laws and the laws of the country.

Muslims living in non-Muslim countries are sometimes torn between the need to keep the laws and customs of the country, and the desire to follow Islam.

Islam teaches that all life is created by Allah and so should be respected. This affects all aspects of Muslim life and involves many social responsibilities. Family life is very important in Islam, and anything which threatens it, such as the possibility of affairs outside marriage, is to be avoided. For this reason, men and women are expected to act and dress modestly and, in some cultures, they are not allowed to mix freely.

Some Muslim women cover their whole body including their face when outside the home. This practice is said to protect them from unwanted male attention and to allow them to be respected for who they are, not how they look.

## Islamic dress code

Men must be covered from the navel to the knee. For women, acting and dressing modestly is called *hijab*. It includes covering the head, arms and legs, but the interpretation of the rules varies.

*Some Muslim women in western countries wear western clothes, but often choose styles that cover their legs and upper arms.*

*Many Muslim women wear head scarves, and plain, loose-fitting long-sleeved clothes to hide the shape of their body.*

*Some women wear a veil to hide the lower part of the face. Clothes are often black, so as not to draw attention to the wearer.*

*This woman is wearing a* burkha, *which covers everything but her eyes. Some* burkhas *have a mesh screen to hide the eyes too.*

## Food laws

In Islam, meat must be prepared in a certain way for it to be *halal* (permitted). The name of Allah is said as the animal is killed, and its blood is allowed to drain away. The *Qur'an* forbids Muslims to eat pork, which is thought to be an impure food. Alcohol is also forbidden, as being drunk makes people forget their duties to Allah, for example, prayer.

## The Jihad

The inner struggle a person has to live a good life is called the *Jihad*. For many Muslims, it includes the holy duty to try to win others over to Islam by setting a good example.

## Birth customs

As soon as possible after the birth of a baby, the father whispers the call to prayer in the baby's right ear. From that moment on, the child is a Muslim.

Seven days after birth, the baby has a name-giving ceremony called 'Aqiqah. Babies are often named after Muhammad or a member of his family, or given another name which has a meaning that is a reminder of the Islamic faith. The baby's hair is shaved off and weighed. Traditionally its weight is given in silver to the poor, but now money is often given instead.

Muslim boys are circumcised (a small piece of skin is cut from the end of the penis). This is not required by the Qur'an, but is a custom that came from the time of Ibrahim, and is a sign of the promise between him and God.

## A Muslim upbringing

Muslim children are taught about their faith from an early age. There is no specific coming of age ceremony, but several significant stages on the way to adult faith are marked. In some countries, children around the age of four have a ceremony called the Bismillah, at which they recite the first few verses of the Qur'an. Another important stage that might be marked is the first time a person fasts at Ramadan, usually as a teenager.

These boys in Kotah, India, are being taught to read the Qur'an in its original Arabic.

## Marriage ceremonies

In some Muslim families, parents choose a marriage partner for their son or daughter, although either partner can refuse if they aren't happy with the match. The formal offer of marriage and its acceptance have to be witnessed by at least two people. Local wedding customs vary, but some common ones are described below.

*The ceremony itself is conducted by an imam and may take place at the bride or groom's house, or at the mosque.*

*The couple kneel hand in hand before the imam. They each confirm that they are marrying willingly and with understanding.*

*During the ceremony there are readings from the Qur'an, usually followed by prayers and a blessing.*

*A wedding contract is signed, and the groom gives the mahr to the bride. This can be jewels, money or other gifts.*

## Death rites

A dying Muslim tries to recite the Shahadah, or if this is not possible, it is said by friends or family instead. After death, the body is ritually washed by members of the same sex and then wrapped in a white sheet called an ihram. Muslims believe that they are all equal so no-one should be buried in better quality cloth than anyone else.

The body is placed on its right side in a coffin, which is buried so that the person faces Makkah. Muslims are always buried, never cremated. The burial takes place at the earliest opportunity, if possible on the day of death. Muslim graves are covered with a mound of earth, and perhaps a plain stone carved with the person's name.

In some countries, the dead person's family observe a 40-day period of mourning. During this time, they do not cook, and they read the Qur'an from beginning to end as many times as they can as a gift to the dead person. On the anniversary of the death, they read the Qur'an through once in memory of the person.

INTERNET LINKS

For links to websites that tell you more about the life of Muslims today, and Islamic rituals of birth, marriage and death, go to **www.usborne-quicklinks.com**

77

# Islamic calendar

The Islamic calendar is dated from the *Hijrah*, Muhammad's journey to Madinah. The letters AH written after a date mean "*Anno Hegirae*" or "year of the *Hijrah*". During the year 2000CE, Muslims witnessed the start of the year 1421AH.

The Islamic year has twelve lunar months. These are based on the cycles of the Moon.

The Islamic year is about 11 days shorter than the solar year (the time it takes the Earth to travel once around the Sun), on which the Gregorian (Western) calendar is based. This means that festivals fall on a different solar date each year.

For Muslims, a month begins at sunset on the day when the crescent moon is first seen. As this depends on where the observer is, and the weather, it is difficult to say exactly when a new month will start.

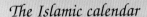

## The Islamic calendar

| | |
|---|---|
| 1st month | Muharram |
| 2nd month | Safar |
| 3rd month | Rabi al-Awal |
| 4th month | Rabi al-Thani |
| 5th month | Jumad al-Ula |
| 6th month | Jumad al-Thani |
| 7th month | Rajab |
| 8th month | Shaban |
| 9th month | Ramadan |
| 10th month | Shawal |
| 11th month | Zul-Qida |
| 12th month | Zul-Hijja |

# New year festival

Shiite Muslims celebrate the beginning of the new year with a ten-day festival called *Muharram*, which shares its name with the first Islamic month. The last and most important day is *Ashura*. The events below are believed to have taken place on *Ashura*.

On the holy day of *Ashura*, Shiite Muslims take part in historical reenactments of the life of the *caliph* Hussein. This man is drawing his mock-sword during one such battle.

*Allah created the heavens and the Earth. He also created Adam who entered Paradise.*

*Noah's ark, carrying two of every living creature, found dry land after a flood that had drowned the Earth.*

*Moses led the Israelites out of Egypt where they had been kept in slavery under the Pharaoh.*

*Muharram* is particularly important to Shiite Muslims. For them it is a time when they mourn the deaths of the *caliphs* Ali and Hussein. On the tenth day, many Shiites dress in black and take part in solemn processions. Some act out passion plays telling the story of Hussein and the massacre at Karbala in which he was killed.

## Two main festivals

The two main festivals during the Islamic year are *Eid ul-Fitr* and *Eid ul-Adha*. *Eid*, or *Id*, is the Arabic word meaning "festival".

On both *Eids*, many Muslims get up early, bathe and put on new clothes and perfume before going to the mosque. There they pray, then listen to the *imam* give a sermon. The prayers on these occasions are slightly different from usual and they may last longer.

After worship at the mosque has ended, people visit their friends and family. They exchange presents and cards, and share celebratory meals.

### Breaking the fast

*Eid ul-Fitr* means "Festival of the Breaking of the Fast". It takes place on the first day of *Shawal*, and celebrates the end of the ninth month, *Ramadan*. The pictures below show how Muslims observe *Ramadan*.

*All healthy Muslims over the age of 12 must fast (eat nothing) between dawn and dusk.*

*They break their fast each evening with a single date, a pinch of salt and a sip of water.*

*The breaking of the fast is followed by prayers and then a family meal called* iftar.

These Muslim women have gathered inside the Dome of the Rock in Jerusalem to say prayers on *Eid ul-Fitr*, the morning after the end of *Ramadan*.

In Muslim countries, *Eid ul-Fitr* is a public holiday. Muslims go to the mosque to thank Allah for his help during the fast, and for his many blessings including the *Qur'an*, which is said to have been revealed to Muhammad during *Ramadan*. *Eid ul-Fitr* is a time for acts of kindness, and in particular, giving money and food to the poor.

### Festival of Sacrifice

*Eid ul-Adha*, the "Festival of Sacrifice", is the most important event in the Islamic calendar. It takes place in *Zul-Hijja*, the last month of the year. *Eid ul-Adha* is celebrated at the end of the religious pilgrimage, the *Hajj* (see page 71) by all Muslims except those on *Hajj*.

At *Eid ul-Adha* an animal is ritually slaughtered and the meat shared with the poor.

*Eid ul-Adha* recalls an event reported in the *Qur'an* and also, in slightly different versions, in the *Torah* and the *Old Testament*. Ibrahim was asked by God to sacrifice his beloved son, Isma'il to show his obedience. Just as Ibrahim was about to kill Isma'il, God provided a ram to take Isma'il's place. The festival celebrates Ibrahim's faith and God's mercy.

### Muhammad's birthday

Some Muslims celebrate the birth of Muhammad, called *Milad-an-Nabi*. This falls on the twelfth day of *Rabi al-Awal*.

In some Muslim countries, *Milad-an-Nabi* is a public holiday, and Muslims celebrate the festival in many ways. Stories of Muhammad's life may be told to encourage people to think about his life and deeds. There may be readings from the *Qur'an*, prayers and sacred songs. Some people decorate their homes, wear festive clothes and hold processions, and feasts at which sweet foods are served.

---INTERNET LINKS---
For links to websites where you can find out more about the Islamic calendar and ways that Islamic festivals are celebrated around the world, go to
**www.usborne-quicklinks.com**

# SIKHISM

Sikhism was founded about 500 years ago by a man who was to become known as Guru Nanak. The word *guru* means "teacher". People who follow Sikhism are called Sikhs, which means "disciples". Today, there are about 27 million Sikhs spread throughout the world. Most live in the Punjab region in northwest India, which is where the religion first began.

This Sikh child is wearing a ceremonial turban for a festival celebration at the Golden Temple, in Amritsar, India. The silver symbol pinned to the turban is known as the *khanda*. It represents Sikh unity.

## History of the Punjab

Starting in the eleventh century, successive groups of Muslims invaded India, which was a mainly Hindu country. Their main route went through a fertile, agricultural region called the Punjab, and some of the invaders decided to settle there. As a result, at the time when Guru Nanak was born, Hindus and Muslims were living side by side.

The map above shows the Punjab region.

Muslim invaders, who were called Moguls, went on to rule over all of northwest India. Their rule continued until the nineteenth century, when the British took over.

In 1947, India became independent of British rule, and the new country of Pakistan was formed. This was in response to demands from Muslims for their own homeland and meant that the Punjab was divided between India (Hindu) and Pakistan (Muslim). Sikhs and Hindus who found themselves living in Pakistan were forced to leave. Many moved to India but others journeyed to countries such as the USA and Britain, taking their religions with them.

## Guru Nanak

Nanak was born in 1469 in the village of Talwandi, near Lahore, in the Punjab. His parents were Hindus but he grew up among both Hindus and Muslims.

When he was 30 years old, Nanak disappeared for three days and everyone thought that he had drowned. When he returned, his first words were: "There is neither Hindu nor Muslim, so whose path shall I follow? I shall follow God's path." By this he meant that the truth of all religions was the same. He believed that the outward differences between religions were unimportant to God.

The man in the painting below is Guru Nanak. He chose to dress in a way that stopped people from easily identifying him as either a Hindu or a Muslim.

┌ INTERNET LINKS ┐
For links to websites where you can find out more about the history of Sikhism and the life of Guru Nanak, go to **www.usborne-quicklinks.com**

Guru Nanak believed that what God had told him was a new message that did not follow on from either Islamic or Hindu teachings. He spent the rest of his life as a teacher, sharing this message. He is said to have made a point of journeying to teach in both Hindu and Muslim holy places.

The Guru spent his last years in the Punjabi town of Kartarpur. Many people came to visit him and learn from his wisdom. From this point on, those who lived as his followers, or disciples, were known as Sikhs. In Kartarpur they formed a community that was friendly to everyone and opened a kitchen to feed the poor and needy.

Nanak died in 1539. One legend describes a disagreement among his followers after his death. His followers with a Hindu background wanted to cremate (burn) his body according to their custom. His Muslim followers wanted his body to be buried.

When the time came to dispose of the body, Nanak's followers found that it had vanished into thin air and only the covering sheet remained.

81

## Sikh beliefs

Sikhs believe in one God. They worship God by living honestly and caring for others. Devoted Sikhs also begin each day at dawn by washing, and reflecting on the Gurus' teachings.

Sikhs believe that the soul goes through cycles of birth and rebirth. To stop this cycle, and merge with God, Sikhs lead disciplined lives, often working in jobs which are good for society. They try to help others (this is called *sewa*), and give a tenth of their income to those in need.

## Nanak's teachings

In his teaching, Nanak stressed the idea that everyone was equal in God's eyes. He taught that the caste system in India, which put some groups of people above others, was wrong.

Nanak often explained his ideas and beliefs through stories. On the right, you can read a story which Nanak told to his followers to illustrate his belief that people should make an honest living for themselves, without exploiting others.

*On a visit to a village, Nanak refused an invitation to dine with a rich merchant. He chose instead to eat with a poor man named Lalo.*

*The rich man was furious. To explain himself, Nanak went to the rich man's house, and took a handful of bread from the table.*

*He squeezed the rich man's bread. As he did so, to the surprise and horror of the merchant, drops of blood spurted out.*

*Nanak then asked for some bread from Lalo, and squeezed it. This time, pure milk ran out. The onlookers were amazed.*

*Nanak explained that although Lalo was poor, he was honest. By contrast, the rich man's wealth had been gained by causing suffering to others.*

## Nanak's successors

When Nanak was near death, he chose one of his followers, a man named Lehna, to succeed him. He changed Lehna's name to Angad which means "part of me". Angad developed a written script for the Punjabi language. It is called *Gurmukhi* which means "from the mouth of the Guru". For almost 200 years, Sikh beliefs were passed down through a chain of Gurus. Each Guru guided the Sikhs by what they did and taught.

This painting shows Guru Nanak praying to God while India was being invaded by the Mogul emperor Babur in 1521.

Guru Nanak was so moved by the brutalities of Babur's invasion of India, shown in the background of this picture, that he spoke out against Babur's tyranny. The fight against political and social injustice is still an important part of Sikh beliefs.

## The community

From time to time during the rule of the Mogul Muslims in India, Sikhs suffered persecution. Both the fifth and ninth Gurus were put to death for their beliefs. The tenth Guru, Gobind Singh, decided to found the community of the *Khalsa* ("the pure"). This was to be a group of loyal Sikhs, who were prepared to resist oppression and defend their faith, by the sword if necessary.

*During a festival in 1699, Gobind Singh's followers were summoned to Anandpur.*

*Upon arrival, they found their Guru standing outside a large tent with his sword drawn.*

*Gobind Singh asked for volunteers who would die for their faith. One man came forward and was led into the tent.*

*The crowd outside the tent heard a sickening thud and Gobind Singh reappeared with his sword covered in blood.*

The story of Gobind Singh, above, goes on to tell how four more men came forward one by one and entered the tent. The Guru then reappeared with all five men alive and well. The men were anointed with a mixture of sugar and water, called *amrit*. They drank the mixture and some was sprinkled on their heads.

These men are dressed in the yellow robes of the *Panj Piare*. Five *Khalsa* Sikhs represent the *Panj Piare* at any festival or parade.

The five men were dressed in yellow robes, and Gobind Singh declared them to be *Panj Piare*, the Beloved Five. They were the first members of the new community, the *Khalsa*. To show equality within the *Khalsa*, the Guru was also initiated into the *Khalsa*. The crowd was inspired by their example and thousands were also anointed, and gained full membership of the *Khalsa*.

Many Sikhs, of both sexes, continue to choose to be initiated into the *Khalsa*. You can find out more about this ceremony on page 86.

## The Holy Book

The last living Guru, Gobind Singh, decided not to select a person to succeed him as Guru. He felt that this would go against the principles of equality that he had tried to promote through the *Khalsa*. Instead, he said that the Sikh scriptures were to be the Guru that would guide all future followers of the Sikh religion.

The Sikh scriptures are gathered together in a book called the *Adi Granth*. Guru Gobind Singh named it the *Guru Granth Sahib* to show its high status. Sikhs treat the book with the utmost respect, but they do not worship it.

The scriptures are made up mainly of hymns, written by the Gurus, expressing Sikh beliefs. The *Guru Granth Sahib* also contains the writings of people from other faiths, including Muslims and Hindus. This is unusual for the main holy book of a religion and shows the respect that Sikhs give to other faiths.

*A page from the Guru Granth Sahib*

**INTERNET LINKS**

For links to websites where you can learn about Sikhism today, the Sikh holy book, the *Gurmukhi* script, and the *Khalsa*, go to **www.usborne-quicklinks.com**

83

The *gurdwara* Harimandir Sahib in Amritsar, in the Punjab, is an important place of pilgrimage. It is surrounded by a lake, from which the city takes its name: Amritsar means "pool of nectar".

## Sikh temples

Most Sikhs go to the temple to worship. A Sikh temple is called a *gurdwara*, which means "door to the Guru". Sikhs can also worship at home, if they have a copy of the *Guru Granth Sahib*.

The *gurdwara* is an important meeting place for the Sikh community. It contains meeting rooms for discussions, and classrooms where Sikh children can learn about their history and faith. Children living outside the Punjab can also learn to speak Punjabi at the *gurdwara*.

Many *gurdwaras* are open all day and night to people of all religions. They also provide a meal and a place to sleep for anyone who needs it.

Every *gurdwara* has a dining room called a *langar*. As well as providing food for those in need, Sikhs always serve a meal after worship. Food, or money toward the cost of the meal, is given by people attending the worship. Both men and women prepare the meal, and vegetarian food is served so that people of all religions can eat together.

## Sikh flag

Most *gurdwaras* have the Sikh flag, called the *Nishan Sahib*, flying outside the building. It is an orange cloth with the *Khanda* symbol (see right) in the middle. The flagpole is also covered with an orange cloth. The *Nishan Sahib* and the flagpole covering may be changed on the third day of a festival called *Baisakhi*.

Sikhs show the *Nishan Sahib* great respect. This is because it represents the unity of Sikhs across the whole of the world.

*This symbol, called the Khanda, represents many of the central Sikh beliefs.*

*The circle, without beginning or end, is called the Chakra. It represents eternity and Sikh unity.*

*The crossed swords are a reminder to Sikhs that they should be prepared to defend their faith.*

*The double-edged sword, the Khanda, represents the power of truth and gives the entire symbol its name.*

The Sikh flag is usually orange with a black symbol. It symbolizes the unity of all Sikhs and so is shown great respect.

The *gurdwara* Harimandir Sahib is often called the Golden Temple.

## Worship

Sikhs do not have a holy day of the week set aside for worship, and can go to the *gurdwara* on any day. The pictures below show some of the things they do there.

*Everyone must cover their head, take off their shoes and wash before entering the prayer room.*

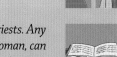

*Everyone sits on the floor as a sign of equality. Men and women, however, often sit separately.*

*There are no priests. Any Sikh, man or woman, can read from the scriptures and lead the worship.*

Guru Nanak felt that elaborate rituals were unnecessary, so Sikhs don't have a set form of worship. Congregational worship is made up of *Katha*, the reading of holy hymns and their explanations from the *Guru Granth Sahib*, and *Kirtan*, the singing of the hymns.

### INTERNET LINKS

For links to websites where you can find out more about Sikh temples and forms of worship, and see pictures of the Golden Temple in Amritsar, go to **www.usborne-quicklinks.com**

During worship, the *Guru Granth Sahib* is placed on a platform. This raises it above the people and gives it the same status as a living Guru. During the day, a canopy hangs over the book and at night the book is moved into a special room. Whenever it is moved, the *Guru Granth Sahib* is always carried above the head as a sign of respect.

At the end of worship the final prayer is always the *Ardas*, or common prayer, which has three parts. The first part remembers God and the Gurus, the second is for the *Guru Granth Sahib*, and the final part asks for God's blessing on the community.

After the prayer, *karah parshad* is prepared, and shared by the congregation. This is a sweet food made with flour, sugar and butter, and stirred with a short sword called a *kirpan*. It is followed by a shared meal in the *langar*.

*Like this man, all Sikhs bow to the Guru Granth Sahib upon entering the gurdwara.*

## Non-stop reading

On occasions such as births, deaths and holy festivals, there is a non-stop reading of the entire *Guru Granth Sahib* called an *Arkhand Path*. This takes about 48 hours. The custom developed in the eighteenth century, when groups of Sikhs were fighting for their faith, and living as outlaws. There were few copies of the book so each group read as much as possible before it was taken to the next group.

The *Guru Granth Sahib* is fanned during readings as a sign of respect. When it is not in use, the book is covered with silk cloths.

Box for money offerings

85

## Sikh sayings

Below are some sayings from Sikhism, with names of the people who said them or the scriptures from which they are taken.

*God is the fish and the fisherman, the water and the net, the float of the net and the bait within it.*
                    Guru Nanak

*Let no-one be proud of their birth. Know that we are all born from the same clay.*
                    Guru Nanak

*He who sings His praises and does good actions will merge into Him.*
                    Guru Amar Das

*A life devoid of love is a flower blooming in the wilderness, with nobody to enjoy its fragrance.*
                    Guru Granth Sahib

*As you sow, so you shall reap. This body is the result of your actions.*
                    Guru Arjan Dev

*Of woman are we born, of woman conceived.*
*To woman engaged, to woman married. Woman we befriend, by woman do civilizations continue.*
*When a woman dies, a woman is sought for.*
*It is through woman that order is maintained.*
*Then why call her inferior from whom all great ones are born?*
                    Guru Nanak

*God is One and eternal. He is to be found in all things and is the sustainer of all things. He is creator and to be found in creation. He is without fear or enmity. He is timeless and beyond birth and death. He is known through God's grace.*
        The Mul Mantra, or statement of Sikh beliefs, that begins the Guru Granth Sahib

## Birth customs

A few days after birth, a Sikh child is taken to the *gurdwara* (temple) for *Nam Karan*, the naming ceremony. At the *gurdwara* the *Guru Granth Sahib* is opened at random and the child is given a name beginning with the first letter of the first word on the left-hand page.

The letter, and sometimes the child's name, is announced to the congregation, and *amrit*, a mixture of water and sugar, is placed on the child's lips. Prayers are said and hymns are sung. On this occasion, the ingredients for the *karah parshad* are provided by the parents.

## Initiation ceremony

Sikhs of both sexes, who are more than about 14 years old, can choose to join the *Khalsa* (see page 83). If they do, they take part in a ceremony based on the original initiation of the Beloved Five. This is called the *Amrit* ceremony. It is led by five outstanding members of the community, who represent the original Beloved Five.

When Sikhs join the *Khalsa*, they take a new name. Men are known as Singh, which means "lion", and women take the name Kaur, which means "princess". The new names were originally intended to make everyone equal and to counteract the caste system of Indian society which indicated a person's importance by their name.

Here, one of the representatives of the original Beloved Five is initiating a Sikh man by sprinkling *amrit* (holy nectar) on his head. The *amrit* was prepared in the large iron bowl and stirred with a dagger.

## The five Ks

Guru Gobind Singh told the original brotherhood to wear five symbolic items of dress. Each item begins with the letter K in Punjabi, so they are known as the five Ks. Many Sikhs today, whether or not they are members of the *Khalsa*, wear the five Ks, as a sign of belonging to the Sikh community. Turbans, which are associated with the Sikh faith, are not one of the five Ks but are worn, mainly by men, to keep their long hair neat and tidy. Young boys sometimes cover their hair with a small cloth called a *patka*.

 *Kesh – uncut hair. This shows a Sikh's obedience to God's will by interfering as little as possible with nature.*

 *Kangha – wooden comb. Long hair must be kept neat and tidy. Sikhs wear the comb in their hair, which is often covered, for example by a turban.*

 *Kachera – white shorts that are worn under the clothes. These symbolize purity and modesty, and were practical for people who might have to fight.*

 *Kara – steel bracelet. The circle represents eternity, and the steel symbolizes strength and purity. It is also a reminder to fight only for God.*

 *Kirpan – a symbolic short sword with a curved blade. It reminds Sikhs that they must fight for the truth and defend the weak and oppressed.*

Sikh couples are given garlands at their wedding ceremony.

## Sikh weddings

The Sikh marriage ceremony is called *Anand Karaj*. This means "ceremony of bliss". The wedding can take place anywhere as long as it is in public. To make the contract sacred, the vows between the couple have to be made in the presence of the *Guru Granth Sahib*.

The ceremony itself is very simple. The bridegroom promises to provide for his wife, and the bride promises to accept her new role. The bride and groom walk four times around the *Guru Granth Sahib*, holding a scarf between them. Prayers are said and hymns are sung. Like all Sikh services, it ends with the eating of *karah parshad*. Many couples then share a meal in the *langar* with family and friends.

## Death rituals

Death is viewed by Sikhs as a natural process in the cycle of birth and rebirth. They believe that the soul will either come back to Earth or, if the person has led a good life, merge with God. For this reason, Sikhs do not believe that there is any use for the body after death and so usually burn, or cremate it. In India, cremation often takes place on funeral pyres made of stacks of wood. In the West, it more commonly takes place in a building called a crematorium.

The dead person's ashes are normally scattered into the nearest river. Sikhs discourage the marking of graves, for example with gravestones, because they believe that it may encourage people to worship the dead body. During the funeral ceremony itself, wailing and other public displays of grief are not encouraged because only the body has died, not the soul.

During the days and night following the funeral, the adults of the family read all of the *Guru Granth Sahib*. This reading takes place over ten days. When the four final passages are read, the official mourning period is over and the family shares *karah parshad*.

┌─INTERNET LINKS─┐
For links to websites where you can learn more about Sikh ceremonies and customs, go to **www.usborne-quicklinks.com**

## Sikh festivals

The Sikh religious calendar used to be based solely on the Hindu lunar (Moon) calendar. Attempts are being made to fix this in relation to the Gregorian (Western) calendar and it is now known as the *Nanakshahi* calendar.

A number of Sikh festivals take place throughout the year. Sikhs celebrate some of the same festivals as Hindus but these often have a slightly different meaning. Some of the festivals are described on these pages. You can read more about the Hindu celebrations on pages 22 and 23.

The chart below shows when Sikh months begin in relation to the Gregorian (Western) calendar.

| SIKH MONTH | GREGORIAN DATE |
|---|---|
| Chet | March 14 |
| Vaisakh | April 14 |
| Jeth | May 15 |
| Harh | June 15 |
| Sawan | July 16 |
| Bhadon | August 16 |
| Asu | September 15 |
| Katik | October 15 |
| Maghar | November 14 |
| Poh | December 14 |
| Magh | January 13 |
| Phagan | February 12 |

These Sikhs are staging mock sword fights as part of their annual *Hola Mohalla* festival.

## Hola Mohalla festival

One local festival in Anandpur, in the Punjab, is called *Hola Mohalla*. This is held on the day after the Hindu festival of *Holi*. The first *Hola Mohalla* was organized by Guru Gobind Singh in 1701.

Traditionally the festival was a day of mock battles and military exercises followed by music and poetry competitions. Today there are still displays of horse riding and swordsmanship, as well as religious lectures.

## Baisakhi festival

The *Baisakhi* festival, held in April, is a reminder of the initiation of the original *Khalsa*. Sikhs visit *gurdwaras*, and hold fairs and parades. Many Sikhs choose to be initiated into the *Khalsa* on this day. On the third day, the flagpole outside the *gurdwara* is lowered, uncovered, and washed with water and yogurt. In India, yogurt is thought of as a pure and sacred substance, and this action symbolizes giving a living holy person a bath. The pole is dried, and put back with a new flag.

## Festival of lights

Like Hindus, Sikhs also celebrate at *Diwali* with a festival of lights (see also page 22). For Sikhs it is also a reminder of Guru Har Gobind, who had been imprisoned by a Mogul emperor. Gobind insisted on the release of 52 Hindu prisoners, who were falsely imprisoned with him, before he himself would leave.

On the day of Guru Har Gobind's release in 1619, the Golden Temple at Amritsar was lit up by many lights to welcome him home. Today lights are still lit outside *gurdwaras*, and sweets are given to all. The greatest gathering takes place at the Golden Temple which is illuminated with thousands of lights in remembrance of the event.

Sikhs celebrate the festival of *Diwali* by decorating their homes and temples with lights. Here, the *gurdwara* Anandgarth Sahib at Anandpur in the Punjab, is being prepared for *Diwali*.

## Festivals of the Gurus

*Gurpurbs* are festivals which mark the anniversaries of the Gurus' birthdays, dates of death and when they became a guru. Two particularly important *gurpurbs* are those of Guru Nanak in November and Guru Gobind Singh in January.

The *gurpurb* is celebrated with processions and prayers. The *Guru Granth Sahib* plays a central role and is sometimes carried through the streets. An *Arkhand Path*, which is a non-stop reading of the *Guru Granth Sahib*, is also often held.

┌─ INTERNET LINKS ─┐
For links to websites where you can learn more about the ten Gurus and the traditions of Sikh festivals, go to
**www.usborne-quicklinks.com**

## The ten Gurus

1. *Nanak 1469-1539; the founder of Sikhism.*

2. *Angad 1504-1552; he developed a written script, called Gurmukhi, for the Punjabi language.*

3. *Amar Das 1479-1574; he worked for the equality of all people.*

4. *Ram Das 1534-1581; he founded the holy city of Amritsar.*

5. *Arjan 1563-1606; he built the Golden Temple at Amritsar. He was the first Sikh to be martyred for his faith.*

6. *Har Gobind 1595-1643; the first "warrior Guru"; he led Sikh resistance against the Muslim Mogul rulers.*

7. *Har Rai 1630-1661; he spread Sikhism in the Punjab and throughout the rest of India.*

8. *Har Krishan 1656-1664; the infant Guru, he was the son of Har Rai and died from smallpox aged eight.*

9. *Tegh Bahadur 1621-1675; he was martyred for trying to protect Hindus.*

10. *Gobind Singh 1666-1708; he founded the Sikh community of the pure and chose the book, the Guru Granth Sahib, to succeed him.*

# SHINTO

Shinto, which means "the Way of the Gods", is a Japanese religion which is believed to have a long history. It was an official state religion in Japan between 1868 and 1945 and about 80% of the Japanese population attend Shinto shrines and ceremonies today. It is quite common for a person to have a Shinto wedding but a Buddhist funeral.

The Sun is associated with the goddess Amaterasu, who is believed to be the ruler of all the spirits.

## Shinto gods

Shinto is based on the belief that spiritual powers, called *kami*, exist in the natural world. Any particularly powerful or impressive natural object or being can be seen as a *kami*. A wide variety of *kami* exist in Shinto, as shown below.

*Natural features, such as lakes and hills, are often seen as* kami. *One of the most well known of these is Mount Fuji in Japan.*

*In Shinto, exceptional people are also seen as* kami. *These include all except the last of Japan's emperors.*

## The Sun goddess

The most important *kami* is the Sun goddess, Amaterasu. She is respected as the ruler of all spirits, as the guardian of Japan's people, and as the symbol of Japanese unity.

The goddess Amaterasu

Amaterasu's symbol is the rising Sun. All of Japan's emperors are believed to have been descended from her. She is also said to have created rice fields, invented the art of weaving and taught people how to grow wheat and breed silkworms.

## Places of worship

Followers of Shinto consider nature to be sacred, so their places of worship are often found in beautiful natural settings. Shinto places of worship are called shrines. Each shrine is the home of at least one *kami*. The entrance to a Shinto shrine is always marked by an archway called a *torii*. The inner hall of the shrine, where the *kami* is thought to be present, can only be entered by Shinto priests and priestesses.

Amaterasu's shrine is in the town of Ise in Japan. All believers try to visit this shrine at least once during their lifetime. Amaterasu's shrine is rebuilt every 21 years to make sure that it is in good repair, and so ensure that the *kami* survives within the shrine.

## Worship

People seek support from Shinto and visit shrines to pray for good fortune and to avoid evil spirits. This is particularly important before special events such as opening a business or taking an exam. Followers believe that purity of body and spirit is important, so the main part of Shinto worship is purification, called *harae*.

*People who visit shrines to worship rinse their mouth and wash their hands before entering the prayer hall.*

*Inside the shrine, people make offerings to the kami. These may be anything from rice or dried fish, to a dance.*

Worship also takes place at home and at work. The home is very important to Shinto because it is through family life that its ancient traditions are preserved. Offerings of rice and water are made at a shrine called a godshelf, and prayers are said, often to ancestors. The worship of gods and ancestral spirits is called *matsuri*.

This archway, or *torii*, forms the gateway to a Japanese island shrine. It symbolizes the border between the human world and the *kami* world.

## Shinto sayings

*Even the wishes of an ant reach to heaven.*

Anon

*To do good is to be pure. To commit evil is to be impure.*

Anon

*Those who do not abandon mercy will not be abandoned by me.*

Oracle of the *kami* of Itsukushima

## Shinto writings

There are no official sacred Shinto scriptures, although there are several books that are regarded very highly by its followers. These include *Kojiki* and the *Nihon-gi*, which were written in the eighth century. They contain collections of the spoken stories of ancient Shinto, although in the main they are books about the history, geography and literature of ancient Japan.

## Festivals

Each Shinto shrine has several major festivals each year. These include *Haru Matsuri* (a spring festival), *Aki Matsuri* (a harvest festival), and *Rei-sai* (the major annual festival). Throughout all these ceremonies, the *kami* are celebrated and people ask for their blessings.

On the day of *Rei-sai*, a procession usually takes place. Known as *Shinko-sai*, or the Divine Procession, it includes the carrying of portable shrines through the streets.

INTERNET LINKS

For links to websites where you can find out more about Shinto beliefs, ceremonies and festivals, go to **www.usborne-quicklinks.com**

# CHINESE RELIGIONS

Two important religions to come from China – Taoism and Confucianism – developed in the sixth century BCE. Modern mainland China is a communist country, and officially atheist, but surveys suggest that around one in five Chinese people are members of a religion (Buddhism, Taoism, Islam or Christianity), and around three in five Chinese believe in forces and figures associated with Confucianism and Chinese folk religion.

Legend tells how Lao-tzu left his job as Keeper of the Imperial Archives and rode away on a water buffalo, as shown in this sculpture, to begin a new life in the hills.

## Taoism

Taoism, pronounced "dowism", is based on the teachings written in the *Tao Te Ching*. This book is usually said to have been written by Lao-tzu, but some scholars think that it had several authors. The *Tao* is often translated as "the Way". Taoists believe that it is the underlying spiritual force of the universe, which is present in all things, yet greater than all things.

The *Tao* is constantly changing, just like nature, and the goal of Taoists is to live their lives in tune with the *Tao*. In order to achieve this, followers need to avoid worldly distractions, and live spontaneously. Taoists believe that problems in life, such as disease and other forms of suffering, are the result of not living in tune with the *Tao*.

China has many temples of different religions. This is the Temple of Heaven in Beijing where emperors in the past used to worship heaven and pray for good harvests.

Taoists believe that two opposing forces in the universe come from the *Tao*: the *yin* and *yang*. The *yin's* qualities include darkness and femininity and the *yang's* qualities include brightness and masculinity. They are believed to be the basis of all creation.

*Yin yang symbol*

One of the most important ideas in Taoism is *Wu Wei*. This means acting naturally and not interfering with the process of life: nothing should be forced. A person should let things happen in their own way, rather than trying to control events.

Taoists share some Buddhist and Confucian festivals. The Ghost Festival, for instance, is similar to a Buddhist festival that takes place on the same day.

*The Tao that can be told is not the eternal Tao. The name that can be named is not the eternal name.*
Tao Te Ching

## Confucianism

Confucianism takes its name from the Chinese philosopher, Confucius, who lived in the sixth century BCE. His name was really K'ung Fu-tzu but in the West he became known as Confucius.

The writings of Confucius were originally intended as advice for the rulers of China. These teachings were later developed by his followers, and they also gradually absorbed ideas from Taoism and Buddhism. Confucianism has since spread from China to Korea, Japan, Vietnam and other southeast Asian countries.

> *Rule by the power of moral example.*
> Confucius

Confucius emphasized the importance of people behaving correctly. He thought that society could become perfect if its members worked hard to achieve "beautiful conduct". This involves always being considerate to others and trying to keep harmony and balance in all things by avoiding extreme emotions and actions. Beautiful conduct also includes the worship of ancestors and respect for the family. This was because Confucius believed that family was more important than an individual.

Female dancers in traditional costume perform at a shrine to Confucius at Sungkyunkwan University in Seoul, South Korea. They are celebrating *Sokchonje*, which is a springtime ritual.

Confucius also placed special emphasis on five relationships. He believed that these formed the basis of a stable, happy society. The relationships are those between ruler and subject, father and son, elder brother and younger brother, husband and wife, and the relationship between two friends.

### Is it a religion?

It has sometimes been said that Confucianism is not a religion because it puts more emphasis on becoming a good citizen than on spirituality. It has also never been organized into a religion with priests, and people worship Confucius as a great teacher rather than as a god. Confucius, however, said, "Heaven is the author of the virtue that is in me," in which he saw heaven as a kind of supreme being.

> *Do not do to others what you do not wish done to you.*
> Confucius

A modern statue of Confucius in Singapore

## Worship

Rituals are very important to Confucians and these are often performed in order to strengthen the five relationships. One of the most important rituals is the worship of ancestors, as Confucians believe that the soul still exists after death. They worship ancestors in the home or at special altars in temples, and make offerings of food, drink and money to them. More elaborate ceremonies are often held on the anniversary of an ancestor's death and on other important occasions, such as festivals.

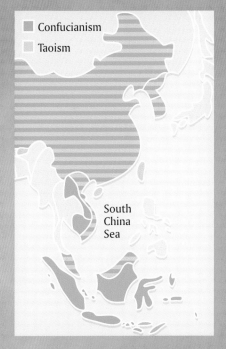

- Confucianism
- Taoism

South China Sea

This map shows the areas in southeast Asia where Taoism and Confucianism are followed, alongside other religions such as Islam and Buddhism.

### INTERNET LINKS

For links to websites where you can find out more about Chinese religions, their writings, places of worship and festivals, go to **www.usborne-quicklinks.com**

# JAINISM

The main figure in the history of Jainism is a man named Mahavira who lived in India in the sixth century BCE. He lived at the same time as the Buddha and is mentioned in Buddhist scriptures. Jains share some beliefs with Hindus and Buddhists. Today, there are about six million Jains, living mainly in India.

## Jain beliefs

Jains believe that every living thing has a soul which is trapped in a constant cycle of birth and rebirth. They believe that they will achieve *moksha*, or release from this cycle, by keeping to three central ideas.

These ideas are known as the three jewels. They are: right belief (in Jainism); right knowledge, through learning about the faith; and right conduct, through following the faith.

Jains do not believe in any kind of supreme being. For them, the universe is without beginning or end, so they do not need to believe in a creator.

*In happiness and suffering, in joy and grief, we should regard all creatures as we regard our own self.*
Mahavira

*First is knowledge, then compassion; that is how the disciplined live. How would an ignorant discriminate between good and evil?*
Dashvaikalik Sutra

*Non-violence is the highest religion.*
Mahavira

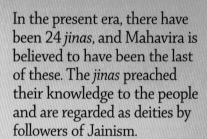

This is an eighteenth-century metal Jain icon. The cut-out shape of the person represents a soul released from the continuous cycle of birth and rebirth.

One way Jains try to seek *moksha* is by showing the greatest respect for all forms of life. The pictures below show how Jains try to achieve this.

*Jains try hard to avoid harming living things, however small, and often sweep insects away from their path.*

*Jains are very strict vegetarians and don't eat root vegetables, as the whole plant dies when its root is pulled up.*

*They also try not to breathe in insects, even by accident, so many Jains cover their nose and mouth with a cloth.*

People who achieve *moksha* while living are called *jinas*. This means "those who overcome". The word *jina* gives the Jain religion its name.

In the present era, there have been 24 *jinas*, and Mahavira is believed to have been the last of these. The *jinas* preached their knowledge to the people and are regarded as deities by followers of Jainism.

## Seeking release

According to Jainism, people's deeds attract *karmas*. Good deeds attract good *karmas* and bad deeds attract bad *karmas*. These *karmas* are attached to the soul and affect what happens to a person in later rebirths.

When the soul finally achieves *moksha*, it is released from the weight of the *karmas* and rises to the top of the universe where it rests in a state of bliss. This state is known as *nirvana*.

## Monks and nuns

Jainism teaches that happiness does not come from material things, so people should have as few possessions as possible. The religion needs great self-discipline and some of its followers choose to become monks or nuns. Many Jains, however, are successful merchants and business people.

In order to become a monk or nun, Jains have to make vows or promises. These include the five great vows of non-violence, telling the truth, not stealing, chastity and giving up their worldly possessions.

One group of monks does not wear any clothes as they have given up all possessions. They are called the *Digambaras*, meaning "sky-clad". Another group, the *Shvetambaras* meaning "white-clad", wears only white robes.

## Pilgrimage

Many important places of pilgrimage are related to the *jinas*. One such place is Pava, where Mahavira died, and many Jains choose to visit Pava at the festival of *Diwali*. On this day, from midnight until early the next morning, pilgrims celebrate the liberation of Mahavira's soul.

There are thousands of Jain temples in India. They are looked after by temple servants. Many Jains visit temples to worship images, such as statues of *jinas* like the ones in this picture. This photograph shows a temple servant performing an act of worship, called *puja*.

## Festivals and rituals

Two important festivals celebrated by Jains are *Diwali* and *Paryushana*. *Diwali* takes place at the same time as Hindu *Diwali* but Jains use the festival to celebrate Mahavira's death and his soul's arrival in *nirvana*. *Paryushana* is an eight to ten-day festival. During this time Jains try to restore to their soul its original virtues such as peace, compassion, and forgiveness.

On the last day of *Paryushana*, an annual rite called *Samvatsari Pratikraman* takes place. On this day, all Jains perform a ritual, known as *Pratikraman*, in which they repent and ask forgiveness for anything that they have done wrong, either intentionally or unintentionally.

*Pratikraman* is performed regularly throughout the year by many Jains, but all Jains have to take part in it at the festival. They believe that if they do not perform *Pratikraman* at least once a year, the *karmas* will become bonded to their soul more strongly than ever, making it harder to shed them and so achieve *moksha*.

┌ INTERNET LINKS ┐
For links to websites where you can learn more about Jainism and see pictures of Jain temples, go to **www.usborne-quicklinks.com**

# THE BAHA'I FAITH

The Baha'i* faith is a new religion which began in Persia (now Iran) in the nineteenth century. It takes its name from a man known as Baha'u'llah, which means "Glory of God". Baha'is see him as the latest and most important in a line of prophets which includes Moses, Krishna, the Buddha, Christ and Muhammad. Today, there are about five million Baha'is worldwide.

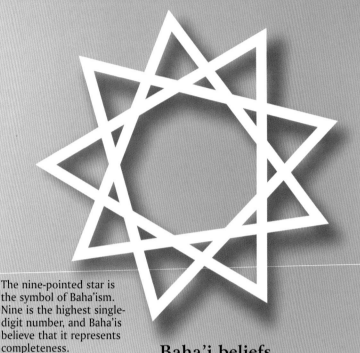

The nine-pointed star is the symbol of Baha'ism. Nine is the highest single-digit number, and Baha'is believe that it represents completeness.

## Historical background

In the nineteenth century, Persia was an Islamic country. In 1844, a merchant named Mirza Ali Muhammad, who was known as the Bab ("gate" to the truth), predicted that a great prophet would come after him. The Bab was seen as a threat to Islam and he was arrested and later executed. A shrine has since been erected to the Bab at Haifa in Israel.

In 1863, Baha'u'llah, the son of a nobleman, proclaimed himself to be the prophet whose coming had been predicted by the Bab. Baha'u'llah was then forced into exile. Under his leadership, those who had previously followed the Bab, and now followed him, broke away from Islam and developed a new religion.

Baha'u'llah believed that it was God's will that he and his followers should try to unite humanity, which he saw as one single race. He believed that the time had finally come for a new world age, with peace, justice and an end to religious and racial prejudice.

Today, Baha'is from many different cultural backgrounds come together at conferences to debate Baha'i laws and issues. These include world unity and the promotion of human rights.

## Baha'i sayings

*Blessed is he who prefereth his brother before himself.*
Baha'u'llah

*The Earth is but one country, and mankind its citizens.*
Baha'u'llah

*So powerful is the light of unity that it can illuminate the whole Earth.*
Baha'u'llah

## Baha'i beliefs

Baha'is believe that all religions share the same god. Baha'u'llah taught that the prophets of different religions, for example Moses, Jesus and Muhammad, spoke the word of this one God. He also believed that the prophets' common purpose was to prepare the human race for the eventual coming together of their different ideas and beliefs in one single religion. Five main Baha'i beliefs are shown below.

1. *Everyone is equal, regardless of sex or race.*

2. *There should be a unity of religions.*

3. *There should be no extremes of poverty or wealth.*

4. *Everyone should be educated.*

5. *True religion should be in harmony with scientific knowledge.*

96
*Baha'i is pronounced "buh-high".

## Baha'i laws

Baha'is believe that life in this world is a preparation for life in a spiritual world after death. They therefore have strict rules and laws on how to behave during their earthly life, to make sure that their soul is ready for life after death. The *Most Holy Book*, which is one of the Baha'i scriptures, contains the laws of Baha'u'llah. Some of these laws are described below.

*Baha'i laws say that believers should pray and meditate daily. They should also not eat during daylight hours on 19 days each year.*

*Baha'is are discouraged from smoking, drinking alcohol and using other drugs because they believe that these deaden the mind.*

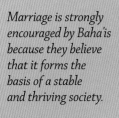

*Marriage is strongly encouraged by Baha'is because they believe that it forms the basis of a stable and thriving society.*

## Worship

The Baha'i calendar is made up of 19 months, each with 19 days. On the first day of each month, there is a feast called the Nineteen-day Feast. This often takes place at someone's home and is the main focus for local Baha'i community worship. The feast is thought of as mainly spiritual, although food and drink are served. The worship includes prayers, readings from scripture, and music. The music often reflects the local culture of the region where the feast is held.

So far, Baha'is have concentrated more on forming communities of followers rather than building temples. Currently, there are seven Baha'i Houses of Worship, spread evenly throughout the world. These are open to people of every religion as places of prayer and meditation: there are no rituals, priests or sermons.

## Pilgrimage

Baha'is in Iran have suffered persecution from various Muslim rulers. They are still discriminated against in Iran, so it is difficult for them to go on pilgrimages to the place of the Bab's home. Bahais also have difficulty visiting the site of Baha'u'llah's home which is in Iraq.

The temple at Haifa, in Israel, which contains the tomb of the Bab (see below).

Today, the headquarters of the Baha'i faith are at Haifa in Israel, where the Bab is buried and where Baha'u'llah visited several times. Baha'is try to visit this site at least once during their lifetime.

**INTERNET LINKS**

For links to websites that tell you more about the Baha'i faith, worship and way of life, go to **www.usborne-quicklinks.com**

Built in 1986, this lotus flower shaped temple in New Delhi, India, is the newest Baha'i House of Worship. Like all other Baha'i Houses of Worship, it has nine sides and a central dome.

# ZOROASTRIANISM

Zoroastrianism was founded in ancient Persia (now Iran) by a philosopher named Zarathushtra or Zoroaster. He is traditionally thought to have lived around 600BCE, although some experts think that he might have lived much earlier. Today, the religion has at least 150,000 followers, who live mainly in Iran and India. Zoroastrians living outside Iran are called Parsis (meaning "Persians").

Zoroaster with a fire symbol. Fire is sacred to Zoroastrians.

## Zoroaster's beliefs

Zoroaster taught that there was only one creator God, Ahura Mazda. This name means "Lord Wisdom". Zoroaster condemned the worship of many gods, a practice that was common in Persia at the time.

According to Zoroastrian teaching, there are two opposing energies within a person's mind. One is believed to create goodness in people, and the other creates evil. Zoroastrians call the positive energy Spenta Mainyu, and the negative energy Angra Mainyu. Zoroastrianism stresses that all people are free to choose between Spenta Mainyu and Angra Mainyu, and that they are responsible for their own actions.

This gold medallion from the fifth century BCE shows a representation of Angra Mainyu, the negative energy which is said to prevent the world from being perfect.

Zoroastrians place their dead within open-topped "towers of silence" like this one in Iran, seen here from inside a nearby building.

By choosing the path of good thoughts, good speech and good actions, Zoroastrians believe that people can make themselves perfect. In doing so they can help to make this world perfect, and so create a true heaven on Earth. In a similar way, the path of evil results in a living hell on Earth.

*Whatever is disagreeable to yourself do not do unto others.*
Shayast-ne-Shayast

## Sacred fire

For Zoroastrians, fire is a symbol of truth, the "Son" of Ahura Mazda. For this reason, fire is treated with respect and a flame is always kept burning in their temples. Zoroastrians often pray in front of a fire, or some other form of light, to help focus their mind on Ahura Mazda.

## The environment

Zoroastrians believe it is important to keep the environment, especially the earth, fire, air and water, unpolluted. For example, the earth (and any nearby water sources) must not be contaminated by the burial of dead bodies, and cremation wastes valuable fuel. Many Zoroastrians therefore follow the custom of putting their dead within isolated, high-walled, open-topped buildings called "towers of silence". There the bodies decay in the Sun's heat. The bones are later buried in a pit.

┌─ INTERNET LINKS ─
For links to websites where you can learn more about Zoroastrianism, go to **www.usborne-quicklinks.com**

# RASTAFARIANISM

Rastafarianism is a very recent religion, founded in the 1930s in Jamaica. Today, the religion has over 100,000 followers. The faith is strongest in Jamaica, but has spread to other Afro-Caribbean communities, particularly in the USA and Europe.

*Rastafarians believe that the Ethiopian emperor, Haile Selassie, is the black Messiah.*

## Historical background

A Jamaican, named Marcus Garvey, foretold that there would be a black Messiah in Africa. When Ras (Prince) Tafari came to the throne of Ethiopia in 1930 as Emperor Haile Selassie, he was hailed as this Messiah.

*Rastafarians often wear items of clothing with the green, yellow and red stripes of the Ethiopian flag.*

*Many Rastafarians wear their hair in long dreadlocks, similar to the hairstyle of ancient African priests.*

*Music is an important part of worship, and the rhythmic reggae style was developed by Rastafarian musicians, such as Bob Marley.*

*Ethiopia shall soon stretch out her hands unto God.*
Bible, Psalm 68

*The ends you serve that are selfish will take you no further than yourself; but the ends you serve that are for all, in common, will take you even into eternity.*
Marcus Garvey

## Rastafarian beliefs

Rastafarians, often called Rastas, accept some of the teachings of the *Bible* because that is the tradition of Ethiopia. They believe that Jah (God) took human form, as Moses, Elijah, Jesus, and finally as Ras Tafari.

As a result of their history of slavery and oppression, Rastas liken the fate of all black people in the West to that of the Israelites, who were enslaved in Egypt (see page 25) and Babylon. They believe that they will not be free until they return to Africa. For many Rastas, Africa is a spiritual state rather than a geographical place. They don't believe in an afterlife, so Africa, and specifically Ethiopia, is seen as heaven on Earth, and is often called Zion.

Rastas try to live as close as possible to nature. Ideally they grow their own food and many are vegetarian, don't smoke tobacco, or drink alcohol or coffee. In some countries, Rastas have come into conflict with the law for their use of the drug cannabis. They see this as a holy herb, and many smoke it as part of their worship.

INTERNET LINKS

For links to websites where you can find out more about what Rastafarians believe and how they live, and listen to some reggae music, go to **www.usborne-quicklinks.com**

The green, yellow and red pattern on this Rastafarian's robes echo the stripes of the Ethiopian flag. The words "freedom" and "redemption" on his staff reflect two goals of Rastafarianism.

# LOCAL RELIGIONS

Since prehistoric times, small groups of people have followed their own local forms of religion. These are often called primal religions – primal means "original" or "first". Most of these religions teach that the world is full of spirits which have an effect on people and the natural world.

This is a shaman's rattle. Shamans often use rattles during their rituals.

## Variations and influences

There are many variations between individual local religions because they are followed in different areas of the world. Many do not have written scriptures, and beliefs are passed on by word of mouth from one generation to the next.

These religions have often come under threat from other, more powerful societies. Some have been destroyed completely while many have been influenced and changed by other faiths. For example, *Santeria*, which is followed by people in the Caribbean, is a mix of African tribal beliefs and Roman Catholicism.

Local religions, however, can also influence the way in which people follow the major religions. In Africa, for instance, local religions influence Christianity and Islam as well as vice versa.

Many local religions use dancing as part of their worship. Dancers, like this one in the Democratic Republic of Congo, Africa, often wear masks and costumes that represent local spirits.

## Shamans

Shamans are important to many local religions. A shaman is a person whose soul is believed to be able to travel to and from the spirit world and communicate with spirit helpers. Shamans believe that these helpers give them the knowledge they need for their work in this world. For example, the advice from such helpers is thought to help shamans cure illness, solve serious problems and even to help prevent natural disasters.

Shamans often use rhythmic drumming, dancing and singing to create a state of mind called a trance. They believe that while they are in a trance, their soul can journey to the world of the spirits. Shamans may also lead ceremonies within the community. These are believed to help build a bridge between the everyday world and the spirit world.

The term "shaman" comes from the Evinki people of Siberia and means "the one who knows". Shamans are mainly found in North and South America, northern Asia, southeast Asia, Indonesia, Japan and Australia. Both men and women can become shamans. Shamans may have been more widespread in the past in some religions that have since died out.

# AFRICA

Traditional African beliefs vary greatly between different groups. They are generally expressed through the telling of myths and through group discussions.

There is a universal African belief in a supreme being who is responsible for creation. Evil is often believed to be produced by spirits, sometimes called tricksters, and by humans who misuse their powers.

Many groups also believe that the supreme being has assistants who help humans. The Yoruba people of Nigeria and Benin call these *orishas*. They believe that there are 401 *orishas* and that each of these has its own special powers.

This South African shaman is holding a "whisk", used to summon spirits. He is wearing furs and a porcupine-quill headdress to increase his powers.

> *God is a great eye. He sees everything in the world.*
>
> Sudanese proverb

Rituals are an important part of African traditional religions. They often involve making offerings to one of the minor spirits in the hope of attracting the spirit's power or help. One reason why people often make offerings to lesser spirits rather than the supreme being is that the supreme being already owns everything in the world.

People often dress up in costumes which reflect how they think a lesser spirit looks. This is done to encourage the spirit they are dressed up as to enter their body.

Today, although the most common religions in Africa are Islam and Christianity, traditional religions like the ones described on these pages are still flourishing.

> *God is like a rich man. You approach him through his servants.*
>
> Igbo proverb

# Vodun

Vodun comes from a word meaning "God" or "Spirit" in the language of the people of Benin. Thousands of Africans, including many of the Yoruba people, were taken to Haiti as slaves. These African slaves combined traditional African beliefs with the Roman Catholic beliefs of the French, who controlled the country at the time. Since 1987, Vodun has been recognized as Haiti's national religion.

All followers of Vodun believe in a supreme being but each group follows slightly different spirits, called *loa*. Rituals are performed to keep these spirits happy, and followers often ask them for good health and good fortune.

Ceremonies are led by priests who can be female or male. The temples always have a pole in the middle which is believed to be where God and the spirits make contact with humans. Vodun is not the same as the fictional "voodoo" shown in many films.

Location of Haiti

INTERNET LINKS

For links to websites where you can discover more about African local religions and their traditions, go to **www.usborne-quicklinks.com**

# AUSTRALIA

The native people of Australia are known as Aborigines. This name means "from the beginning", as they are thought to have lived in Australia for over fifty thousand years.

## The Dreaming

The most important of the Aborigines' beliefs is known as the Dreaming. Aborigines believe that one aspect of the Dreaming is a period of time, known as the Dreamtime, at the beginning of creation. During the Dreamtime, enormous spirit-beings moved across the land. These took many shapes, for example kangaroos and humans, but they are most commonly believed to have been giant serpents.

*As the spirits moved, they shaped the landscape and even gave parts of themselves to it, such as eyes for waterholes and tails for trees.*

*Aborigines believe that these spirits also created all living things, including humans, and the spirits of the people who would be born in the future.*

*Finally, the spirits changed again into forms such as animals, stars and hills. People, animals and the land are therefore felt to be closely related.*

These Aboriginal boys are taking part in a ceremony to mark their change into adults. The patterns painted on their skin are believed to help them grow.

*Wayfarer, there are no paths. Paths are made by walking.*
        Australian Aboriginal saying

The Dreaming is also thought of as a spiritual place. Aborigines believe that if they perform rituals at the places sacred to the spirits, for example specific rocks or trees, they will be able to reach beyond the everyday world to the spirit world.

Sacred places, called Dreaming sites, are very important. Aborigines believe that anyone born near one of these is a human form of the spirit associated with it.

The rock below is known as Ayers Rock or by its aboriginal name, *Uluru*. For centuries, Aborigines have performed rituals inside the caves of *Uluru*, and many of the cave walls are decorated with paintings of the Dreamtime.

## Holy men

Aboriginal holy men, called *Karadjis*, are believed to be in direct contact with the Dreaming and its spirit beings. They sometimes wear feathers on their ankles to symbolize their ability to "fly" to the spirit world. The *Karadjis* are the only people who create new dances, songs and stories about the Dreaming.

## Stories of the Dreaming

The beliefs about the Dreaming are supported by local stories, or myths, which are passed down the generations by word of mouth. The beliefs can also be seen in art which represents these myths.

Instruments, like these clap sticks, are used to accompany the telling of myths.

The myths also describe the local landscape, and how it was created, in enough detail to form spoken maps. Originally, the maps from all the groups interconnected and covered the whole country. Today, only about 1.5% of Australia's population think of themselves as Aborigines. Many of the links between the groups have been broken and some of the local beliefs and knowledge lost.

# PACIFIC ISLANDS

The Pacific region covers about a fifth of the world's surface and is thought to contain at least twenty thousand islands. It is divided into three main areas: Melanesia, Polynesia and Micronesia. Although Christianity is now the main religion of the area, a variety of traditional religions are still followed by the different groups of people living on the islands.

## Creation beliefs

Islanders hold different ideas about the nature of the universe. For instance, the Maoris of New Zealand believe that the universe was not created and that it has no beginning or end.

One figure who is described in different myths across the Pacific region is Maui. He is believed to be a trickster rather than a helpful spirit. Maui's adventures are thought to include the creation of the Pacific islands by dragging them up from the seabed, and the stealing of fire for humans.

This jade symbol is a Maori charm. It is probably worn to ensure good luck and fertility.

## Sacred force

The idea of *mana* is a belief shared by many Melanesians and Polynesians. *Mana* is a sacred force present in all things, whether alive or not. It is particularly great in important people, such as chiefs. Until recently, the chiefs in Tahiti were not allowed to touch the ground when they moved across the country. This was because their *mana* was believed to be so powerful that each patch of earth they made contact with would become a sacred place.

The Maori people of New Zealand worship their ancestors and often carve wooden statues of people like this to show their respect.

## Community rules

To prevent any loss of *mana* from the community, people have created strict rules for behaving. These include rules to stop anyone from entering sacred places because they may destroy the *mana* there.

*The traditional penalty for breaking very important rules, such as touching the head of a chief, used to be death.*

*The punishment for breaking minor rules is believed to be given by the spirits, often in the form of illness or bad luck.*

Most believers simply follow their faith by keeping to the rules and rituals. These rules are called *tabu* (or *tapu*), and it is from this name that the Western word "taboo" stems. A few believers, however, are specially chosen to learn about the religion in greater depth through the telling of myths.

*Feed a man with fish, he will live from day to day. Teach him how to fish, he will live forever.*

Maori saying

─INTERNET LINKS─
For links to websites about the local religions of Australia and New Zealand, where you can listen to myths of the Dreaming, learn to play a didgeridoo and discover more about Maori beliefs, art, language and people, go to **www.usborne-quicklinks.com**

# NORTH AMERICA

The Native Americans, or First Nation People, live in groups known as tribes, whose history goes back at least thirty thousand years. Beliefs vary greatly from one tribe to the next, but they all share a very close relationship with the natural world. This is reflected in many of their beliefs and ceremonies.

*Treat the Earth well: it was not given to you by your parents, it was loaned to you by your children. We do not inherit the Earth from our ancestors, we borrow it from our children.*
First Nation proverb

This Native American woman is holding a ceremonial pipe.

## Sharing the pipe

A ceremony common to all North American tribes involves the smoking of tobacco in a pipe, which is shared among the group. They believe that this ritual links the people in the earthly world to the spirit world, as explained below.

*Tobacco is used because when it is growing, its roots go deep into the ground. This connects it to the earthly world.*

*When the tobacco is burned, however, its smoke rises high into the sky, connecting it to the spirit world.*

*The pipe links the Earth and the sky, and therefore the two worlds. It is treated with great respect.*

## Purification ceremony

A ceremony known as purification is important to tribes such as the Plains People. It is often called a sweat, but it is more spiritual than a simple sauna, and followers see it as a process of rebirth. Purification takes place in and around a circular hut, or lodge, made of branches. The content of the ceremony varies between tribes but there are some similarities.

Before the main ceremony, tribes often perform a ritual known as smudging. Smoke from smouldering sage and sweetgrass is drawn in the direction of a person's heart and over the head. This is thought to release the plants' blessings and replace any negative energies, of a group or individual, with positive ones.

## Inside the lodge

The ceremony is often led by a lodgekeeper or a shaman (see page 100), who forms a link between the spirit world and the everyday world. A number of rocks are heated on a fire outside the lodge, before being carried inside and placed in a pit in the middle of the floor.

*The lodge itself is covered with blankets or other thick cloth, to hold in the heat from the rocks, and block out any light.*

At the start of the ceremony, the rocks are sprinkled with sage to rid the lodge of negative energies. Sweetgrass is placed on the hot rocks. This is believed to summon good spirits to the lodge and to help carry prayers to them. The pictures below show some of the other rituals that can take place during the ceremony.

*Water is thrown onto the hot rocks. As it evaporates, the darkened lodge becomes filled with steam.*

*People offer prayers of thanks and praise to the spirits. They sing sacred songs and ask the spirits for guidance.*

*Only after the last tree has been cut down. Only after the last river has been poisoned. Only after the last fish has been caught. Only then will you find that money cannot be eaten.*
Cree tribal prophecy

## SOUTH AMERICA

In South America, many of the groups which still follow local religions live in rainforests or mountainous regions and have little contact with other cultures. Their relationship with the land and their environment is very important. Many of their rituals and ceremonies are performed to make sure that the balance of nature's cycles is preserved.

Shamans (see page 100) are vital to many of these groups. For example, about a quarter of the men of the Huichol tribe in Mexico are thought to be shamans, and the tribe members call themselves "the healers".

The Warao Indians of Venezuela have three types of shamans. One, the *wisiratu*, use a sacred instrument to help cure illnesses and as part of their rituals. The instrument, called a *hebu mataro*, is a large, hollowed-out fruit filled with pebbles. The Warao believe that the rattling sound it makes is the voice of a helping spirit.

## Spirit world

The belief that the everyday world is part of a larger spirit world is held by many tribes. For example, the Yanomami, who live in the rainforests of Brazil, believe that they have the same relationship with the spirit world as they do with each other.

When hunting or gardening, the Yanomami believe that they are releasing spirits from the plants and animals that they kill. These spirits are believed to seek their revenge by attacking the people during their dreams, often causing illness. They can only be controlled by songs and dances performed by shamans, who call for the aid of spirit helpers.

## ARCTIC REGIONS

Shamans play an essential role in the local religions of countries like Siberia and Alaska. The Buryats of Siberia recognize two sorts of shamans: the "white" shamans, who work with the gods, and the "dark" shamans, who summon the spirits. Many shamans are believed to be able to transform themselves into birds and animals. This is thought to help them travel to the spirit world.

The Inuit people of Alaska traditionally believe in a variety of spirits. The most important of these is Sedna, who is half woman and half seal. Living in the sea, she controls the actions of all sea animals. If she is angry, the Inuit believe that she stops the hunters from catching seals. If she is pleased, however, she provides them with food from the sea. Shamans are thought to be able to influence Sedna on the people's behalf.

INTERNET LINKS

For links to websites about local religions followed today in the Americas and the Arctic, go to **www.usborne-quicklinks.com**

This Siberian shaman is wearing a costume which symbolizes the animal guide he has chosen. He is also holding a drum. Both the drum and the guide are used to help the shaman travel to the spirit world.

# PAST RELIGIONS

Many ancient religions no longer exist. Some died out because the societies which followed them died out. Others died out when people were converted to other religions. Most of what is known about these ancient religions comes from archaeologists' finds. On these and the next few pages, you can read about some religions of the past.

Experts believe that some of the rock paintings, similar to this one, left by the Cro-Magnon people may have been used in religious ceremonies.

## Earliest religions (c.35,000BCE)

Archaeologists think that the Cro-Magnon people, who are believed to be the oldest direct ancestors of modern humans, were interested in the world of the spirit. It is thought that these people were trying to understand the world around them and explain the great forces of nature that could bring plenty or disaster.

Cro-Magnon people carved figures in stone of very fat, often pregnant, women. They also made statues in clay and dried them in the fire. The people may have believed that carvings like these would bring them good fortune.

This figure was unearthed in Austria. It is believed to be about 22,000 years old and is thought to be a fertility goddess.

Many experts think that the cave art of the Cro-Magnon people may have had religious or magical purposes. Their paintings are often found deep within the caves, which perhaps means they were used for secret rituals. Many paintings show animals that are pregnant or pierced with spears. People may have believed that such paintings would increase the fertility of the herds they hunted for food, or strengthen the hunters' power over the animals.

The footprints of both children and adults have been found near some of these painted caves. The paintings may have played a part in initiation rites, in which children had to pass a test to be allowed to enter the cave for the first time and be put in touch with the spirit world.

In the cave of Les Trois Frères in southwest France, there is a rock painting showing a figure clothed in animal skins and feathers and wearing what is thought to be a headdress of reindeer antlers. Some experts believe that this figure is a shaman: a person who was thought to have special powers to communicate with the spirit world.

Archaeologists have found graves in which tools and the remains of food were buried alongside the body. This suggests that the Cro-Magnon people believed in some kind of afterlife in which these things would be needed.

## Early farmers (10,000-5600BCE)

Farming first developed about 11,000 years ago, in the Middle East (now Turkey, Syria, Iran and Iraq). Small stone statues dating from this time suggest that the early farmers believed in a Mother Goddess, who was responsible for the fertility of crops and animals. A young god, whose symbol was a bull, was sometimes associated with her.

Many shrines have been excavated at the ancient town of Çatal Hüyük (in modern Turkey). Wall paintings of religious scenes suggest that some priestesses dressed as vultures and performed rituals. Skulls were found in baskets below plaster bulls' heads.

Some early farmers worked together to create buildings from massive blocks of stone. Around 3200BCE, people in northwest Europe began to build great circles and lines of standing stones called megaliths. These monuments may have been used for religious rites.

The stones below are part of a stone circle, known as the Ring of Brodgar, in the Orkney Islands off the Scottish coast. The circle has been dated to at least 1560BCE. Experts have various theories about the religious rites that may have taken place here.

## Mesopotamia (c.3500BCE-100CE)

Mesopotamia corresponded roughly with modern Iraq. Writing was first developed there in about 3500BCE, so there are records of the beliefs and practices of the various peoples who lived there. These beliefs all involved many deities. Every village was under the protection of a deity who lived in a temple built on a platform. By about 2000BCE, these buildings had developed into huge temple-towers, called *ziggurats*.

Royal graves found at a place called Ur contain the skeletons of dozens of people. It appears that they killed themselves in order to follow their king or queen into the next world.

Statues of three Mesopotamian priests with their hands clasped in prayer

## Minoans (c.2500-1450BCE)

The Minoans lived on the isle of Crete, in the Mediterranean Sea. Goddesses and their priestesses were the main focus of their religion, with male gods playing a lesser role. The Minoans made offerings to deities at mountain shrines or in rooms at large palaces in the main towns.

Wall painting showing a team of bull-leapers

The large palace courtyards were the venue for a dangerous sport known as bull-leaping. Trained acrobats grasped the horns of a charging bull and somersaulted over its back. The bull was sacred to the sea god, so bull-leaping may have been part of a religious rite.

## Canaanites (c.1600-1200BCE)

Canaan lay at the east end of the Mediterranean Sea. Its people had many deities, but the most powerful one was Baal, the god of rain, storms and war. His wife, Asherah, was goddess of love. Priests sacrificed animals and sometimes people at hilltop shrines called "high places".

### INTERNET LINKS

For links to websites where you can see more cave paintings and stone circles and explore the ancient city of Çatal Hüyük, go to **www.usborne-quicklinks.com**

# ANCIENT EGYPT

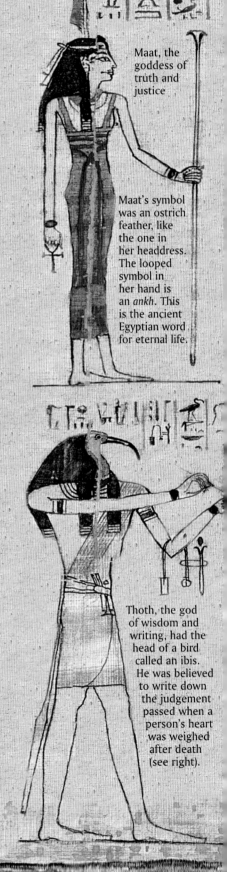

Maat, the goddess of truth and justice

The ancient Egyptian civilization flourished between about 3500 and 30BCE. People had a strong faith in many gods, life after death and the need to live a good life on Earth. These traditional beliefs began to wane in the first century CE, when Christianity became popular in Egypt. Later, in 641, a Muslim invasion converted the country to Islam, which is still its main religion today.

Maat's symbol was an ostrich feather, like the one in her headdress. The looped symbol in her hand is an *ankh*. This is the ancient Egyptian word for eternal life.

## Gods and goddesses

The Egyptians had dozens of gods and goddesses who cared for all aspects of life, death and the Next World, where people hoped to go after they died. Most deities were significant only in the home or in certain villages or towns, but some, such as Re, the Sun god, became nationally important.

Most deities were associated with a particular animal or bird, and were often shown in paintings with the head of that creature. It became the custom for a creature of that species to be kept in the deity's temple. Eventually, some entire animal species, for example, cats, were believed to house a little of the deity's spirit.

From about 2400BCE, kings of Egypt were believed to be gods. The spirit of the god Horus was thought to live in the king, and kings were also said to be descended from the Sun god, Re, who had been the first king of Egypt.

## Temples and festivals

The Egyptians built huge stone temples as earthly homes for their deities. Each temple housed a statue of the deity to whom it was dedicated. This was cared for by priests. Ordinary people never entered the temple, but came to the courtyard to say special prayers.

On festival days, the statue was carried through the streets on a sacred barque (a boat on poles). It was accompanied by priests, dancers and musicians. Anyone could ask questions of the statue. The deity's answer (yes or no) was believed to be shown by how the boat moved: back and forth or pressing down.

Carved statues outside the Temple of Nefertari (the wife of Egyptian ruler Rameses II) and Hathor (the great Mother Goddess) at Abu Simbel, Egypt.

Thoth, the god of wisdom and writing, had the head of a bird called an ibis. He was believed to write down the judgement passed when a person's heart was weighed after death (see right).

## After death

According to Egyptian beliefs, every person had three souls, called *ka*, *ba* and *akh*. For a person's souls to function properly in the Next World, it was thought to be essential for the body to be kept from decaying after death.

Poor people were often buried in shallow graves. Their bodies dried out quickly in the hot sand and were largely preserved from decay. Those who could afford it had their bodies painstakingly preserved by a process called mummification. This involved taking out the internal organs, stuffing the body with linen, salt, sawdust and sweet-smelling spices and wrapping it in bandages. After this process, the body was called a mummy.

This illustration from the *Book of the Dead* shows the jackal-headed god, Anubis, weighing the heart of Anhai (far right) against the Feather of Truth. Anhai is led by the god Horus. Next to Anubis is the monster who ate wicked people whose hearts weighed heavy.

## Funerals and tombs

Egyptian funerals were often grand. A procession of friends and family went with the body to the tomb. Noble families also had professional mourners, priests, animals for sacrifice, and porters who carried the dead person's belongings. At the tomb door, a priest performed an "Opening of the Mouth" ceremony. This was believed to restore the dead person's abilities and powers. The wooden coffin was sealed in a stone coffin called a sarcophagus, then shut in a burial chamber.

The tombs of the wealthiest people were decorated inside with scenes of daily life. This was believed to ensure that these activities carried on after death. The upper chambers of the tomb were usually left open so that regular offerings of food could be left for the dead.

## The Next World

Before entering the Next World, a dead person had to undergo several tests or ordeals. The person needed amulets, and a *Book of the Dead*, containing spells, information and a map, to help bypass the dangers.

*If a person passed all these tests, the heart was weighed against the Feather of Truth.*

*If the person had led a sinful life, the heart would be heavy and the person would be fed to a monster.*

*A good person's heart would balance with the Feather. This person would live happily in the Next World.*

**INTERNET LINKS**

For links to websites where you can learn more about the religious beliefs of the ancient Egyptians and take a tour of the Pyramids, go to **www.usborne-quicklinks.com**

109

# GREECE AND ROME

The civilization of Ancient Greece flourished between 750 and 30BCE. The city of Rome was founded in about 753BCE, and by 100BCE the Romans had a vast empire, which lasted until about 400CE. As the Romans spread beyond Rome, they came into contact with people from many countries, including the Greeks. The Romans matched their own gods to the Greek ones, making them the basis of their state religion.

A Greek vase painting of the princess Europa being kidnapped by the Roman god Jupiter, disguised as a bull.

## Gods and goddesses

The Greeks believed in many gods and goddesses who controlled different aspects of life or death. The 12 most important of the Greek deities were thought to live on Mount Olympus, the highest Greek mountain. Many legends were told to describe the personalities of the deities and what pleased or angered them. The king of the gods was Zeus. He controlled the sky and thunder.

The Greek god, Zeus, with his thunderbolt. Jupiter, the chief Roman god, was the equivalent of Zeus.

Vesta (Hestia to the Greeks) was goddess of the hearth. Every city and home had a shrine dedicated to her. At her shrine in Rome, a fire was kept burning by six women called Vestal Virgins.

As well as the equivalents of the main Greek deities, the Romans also had many other lesser gods, for example Flora and Faunus, who were responsible for growth and fertility. The Romans also believed that their homes were protected by household spirits called *numina*. One group, the *penates*, looked after the stores; another, the *lares*, protected the whole household. Each family also had its own guardian spirit, the *genius*, and ancestral spirits.

From about 44BCE, emperor worship became popular among the Romans. At first, only some emperors were thought of as gods, and then only after their death.

## Mystery religions

People who wanted a deeper religious experience than was offered by the rituals of state religion often turned to mystery cults. These placed more emphasis on living a virtuous life, and some promised life after death. People were trained and initiated by stages into the cult. They could take part in rituals, rather than just watch them.

The most famous Greek mystery cult was that of the goddesses Demeter and Persephone at Eleusis. In the Roman world, the all-male cult of the Persian god Mithras became popular, especially with soldiers. The cult of the Egyptian goddess Isis also gained many Roman followers.

Demeter, goddess of plants and harvests

## Messages from the gods

The Greeks and Romans had a strong belief in the supernatural. They used many methods to try to predict the future and learn the gods' will. The Greeks, for example, might visit an oracle, where a priest or priestess could speak on behalf of a god. The most famous oracle was at Delphi. There the god Apollo was believed to speak through his priestess, the Pythia. Some Roman ways of foretelling the future are described below.

*Special priests called* haruspices *examined the livers of sacrificed animals. The liver's condition was said to show the gods' will.*

*In Rome, a group of 16 prophets called* augurs *predicted the future by observing flocks of birds, cloud shapes and lightning.*

*In a national crisis, three books of prophecies, written by a prophetess called the Sibyl, were consulted. These were kept closely guarded.*

*The Parthenon in Athens was a temple dedicated to the Greek goddess Athene, who was responsible for wisdom and war, and was patron goddess of Athens. The Romans adopted the Greek idea of using rows of columns in many of their own temple designs.*

## Temples and worship

Both the Greeks and the Romans built impressive temples to be the homes on Earth of their state deities. Each temple had an inner room, or sanctuary, which housed a statue of the deity. Only priests were allowed in there. Ceremonies took place outside the temple. People brought animals or birds as offerings to the deity. These were sacrificed by a priest at a stone altar.

Many religious festivals were held during the year to please the deities and persuade them to grant people's wishes. As well as religious ceremonies, with prayers, sacrifices and processions, these festivals often included events such as athletics, poetry and drama competitions.

Daily family worship in the home also played an important part in Greek and Roman religions. This involved saying prayers and making offerings to the household gods.

## Life after death

Roman beliefs about life after death were, on the whole, vague. Most thought that the afterlife was dull and boring. The Greeks believed that after death, the soul went to one of three places in Hades, the kingdom of the dead.

*Very virtuous souls were sent to the Elysian Fields, a happy place full of sunshine, warmth and laughter.*

*Most people, who had been neither very good nor very bad, went to a drab, misty place called the Asphodel Fields.*

*People who had lived wicked lives were flung into Tartarus, a place of eternal torture, torment and misery.*

## INTERNET LINKS

For links to websites where you can discover more about the religions of ancient Greece and Rome, and read stories about their gods and goddesses, go to **www.usborne-quicklinks.com**

# NORTHERN EUROPE

The religions of the Celtic, Germanic and Norse people began in northern Europe. Beliefs were passed on by word of mouth, so much of our knowledge comes from the writings of people, such as the Greeks, Romans and Christian missionaries, who were hostile toward them or misunderstood them. These reports were therefore biased against them. Some people still have beliefs based on these ancient religions.

## Ancient Celtic beliefs

The Celts were a warrior people who emerged in eastern Europe in about 1000BCE. By the fourth century BCE, they occupied much of Europe, but by the first century CE, most of the Celtic territories had been conquered by the Romans.

There appear to be about 300 different Celtic deities, but experts think that many of these are local variations. For example, Lancelot, Lleu and Lug are probably all aspects of the same original Sun god, who was the chief deity of Celts everywhere.

The Celts believed that after death, a person's soul was taken to the Otherworld. There, life carried on and ended the same as it did in this world. After the person died in the Otherworld, the soul came back to this world and lived again in another human body. For this reason, at every birth, Celts mourned the death of the person in the Otherworld who had made the new birth possible.

## Sacred wells

Wells were particularly important to the Celts because they were thought to link this world to the Otherworld. The Celts believed that the Well of Wisdom stood in the middle of the Otherworld and that this was the source of all the spiritual wells in this world.

Many wells were associated with particular deities. People visited sacred wells hoping to find wisdom or a cure for an illness. They left offerings in return. People often only visited wells in May or at Midsummer because the gates to the Otherworld were believed to be wide open at these times.

The photograph on the right shows a Celtic stone cross in Cornwall, England. Christianity gained a strong following among the Celts and absorbed some Celtic beliefs. Some experts think that the Celtic cross, an upright or diagonal cross in a circle, may be a combination of the Christian cross and earlier Celtic symbols.

## Celtic priests

There were three main spiritual groups within the Celtic religion. The most important of these were the Druids, who performed all rituals and made contact with the gods. The Vates or Ovates were philosophers who were also believed to be able to predict the future. The Bards were historians, musicians, poets and singers.

Celebrations of the seasons play an important part in religions based on the old Celtic beliefs. This photograph shows some modern Druids celebrating a Midsummer festival at Stonehenge in England.

## Celtic rituals

The Druids often conducted rituals in sacred groves of trees. Some rituals marked life stages, such as naming ceremonies at birth. Others celebrated changes in the seasons. The main ones were *Samhain* (November 1st), *Imbolc* (February 1st), *Beltane* (May 1st) and *Lughnasad* (August 1st). *Samhain* marked the Celtic new year and probably involved a remembrance of the dead.

According to Greek and Roman authors, some rituals involved human sacrifices. The Celts also collected human heads after battle. The Celts believed that the head was the site of the soul, and that the head could live even after being removed from the body.

The Celts believed that some of their gods lived in streams, rocks and trees. As shown here, Druids threw precious objects into sacred pools as gifts to the gods.

## Northern religions

The ancient Germanic people, and the Norse people (who lived in Scandinavia, Iceland and Russia), flourished between about 700BCE and 1100CE. They believed that gods and goddesses affected every aspect of their lives, for example, agriculture, fishing and war. They told stories, called sagas, about the lives and adventures of their gods and goddesses.

According to Norse legend, Odin, the chief Norse god, rode an eight-legged horse.

One of the most important gods in the sagas was Odin, also known as Wotan or Woden. He was king of all the gods and the creator of the world and all living things. Odin was always shown with one eye as he gave the other in return for a wisdom-giving drink from a well. His wife was Frigg, queen of the deities, and goddess of love and death. She cared for all people, especially women and children.

## Norse worship

Little is known about how the Norse people followed their religion. It is thought that they built temples, but because these were made from wood, very few remains have survived.

## The Norse universe

According to Norse beliefs, the universe was made up of three levels, arranged on top of each other. The trunk of an ash tree, known as the World Tree or *Yggdrasil*, passed through all three levels.

*On the top level were the worlds of* Asgard *and* Vanaheim, *where the gods and goddesses lived.*

*In the middle was* Midgard, *the world of humans, and the worlds of the Giants, Dwarves and Dark Elves.*

Muspellheim, *the Land of Fire, and* Niflheim, *the icy Land of the Dead, were on the lowest level.*

*Niflheim* was a place of ice and darkness ruled by Hel, the Queen of the Dead. Norsemen who died from sickness or old age passed into Hel's land. The souls of those who died in battle were taken by warrior women called *Valkyries* to *Valhalla*, Odin's feast hall in *Asgard*.

┌─INTERNET LINKS─┐
For links to websites where you can find out more about ancient religions of Northern Europe, delve into Norse myths and learn about the beliefs of the ancient Celts, go to **www.usborne-quicklinks.com**

113

# EARLY AMERICA

Several civilizations developed in Central and South America between 1000BCE and 1500CE. The greatest of these were the Mayas, the Incas and the Aztecs. Experts believe that for these people, religion was a powerful force that affected everything they did. In the sixteenth century, Spanish explorers arrived, bringing Christianity with them. The American empires were destroyed through wars with the Spaniards and by the diseases the invaders brought with them. A few people still follow religions based on some of these original ideas.

This is a ceremonial knife. Its handle is decorated with an Inca god.

SOUTH AMERICA

This map shows the Mayan, Aztec and Inca Empires.
- Mayan Empire (c.250-900CE)
- Inca Empire (c.1200-1530)
- Aztec Empire (c.1325-1520)

## The Incas

The Incas were a farming people, so their religion revolved around the worship of the Sun, Inti, who gave warmth to their crops. Other important deities were Mamquilla (the Moon), Pachamama (Mother Earth) and Illapa (the Thunder or Rain Giver).

The rulers of the Incas were known as Sapa Incas. Each ruler claimed to be the son of the Sun in order to reinforce his power. When a Sapa Inca died, it was said that the Sun had recalled him. People would worship the dead rulers as ancestral gods. Ancestors were very important and the Incas regularly visited tombs and consulted the dead for help.

## Sacred places

Inca sacred sites were called *huacas*. One of these was the Temple of the Sun in the city of Cuzco. Inside the temple, there were gold images of the Sun, often shown with a human face. Mountains were important *huacas* as they represented a way to get closer to Inti. The Incas are believed to have made sacrifices, usually of animals, on top of the mountains to please the gods and to ensure rain, good crops and protection. Archaeologists recently found the frozen remains of some people on the top of several mountains. They were specially chosen Inca children, who were sacrificed to be messengers between the Incas and Inti.

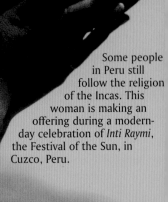

Some people in Peru still follow the religion of the Incas. This woman is making an offering during a modern-day celebration of *Inti Raymi*, the Festival of the Sun, in Cuzco, Peru.

## Mayas and Aztecs

The Mayan civilization was at its greatest between 300 and 900CE. The Mayas lived in small kingdoms ruled by powerful kings who were also priests and warriors.

The Aztecs were a wandering people who settled and built a village on an island in Lake Texcoco in about 1200. Known as Tenochtitlan, this village grew to become the capital of the Aztec Empire.

Both the Mayas and the Aztecs built temples in which to worship Quetzalcoatl, the feathered serpent. They both believed that he was the god of knowledge. The Mayas also believed that Quetzalcoatl was the inventor of their calendar, and the Aztecs thought that one day he would appear, to decide their fate.

The Mayas and Aztecs built their temples on the top of pyramids. The temples were the focus of religious worship, where most sacrifices were performed.

The Mayas often buried their kings under temples built on pyramids like these.

This mosaic mask, made from a gemstone called turquoise, shows the Aztec serpent god Quetzalcoatl.

## Mayan beliefs

One of the most important Mayan gods was Ahaw Kin, the Sun god. When the Sun disappeared at nightfall, the Mayas believed that he went to the underworld and became the jaguar god. Jaguars were very important to the Mayas because they were seen as the king of the forest. Mayan kings often wore jaguar furs as a sign of their power.

Carving of a Mayan queen offering blood

As well as ruling, Mayan kings and queens performed religious ceremonies and shed their own blood as an offering to the gods. After death, the kings were buried underneath temples, often wearing masks showing Ahaw Kin's face. The people then prayed to them in the same way as they did to other gods.

## Aztec beliefs

The Sun was very important to the Aztecs. Their leader and most important god, Huitzilopochtli, represented both the Sun and war. Every year, they fought a special war against nearby tribes. In this war, called the War of the Flowers, they captured victims to sacrifice to Huitzilopochtli.

The Aztecs believed that the world had already lived through the destruction of four suns. They made sacrifices to Huitzilopochtli because they believed that the Sun might die again if they did not keep the god strong.

The heart was seen as particularly valuable, so Aztec priests would take the heart of a prisoner and offer it as a sacrifice to Huitzilopochtli. A sixteenth-century Mexican manuscript called the *Codex Magliabecchiano* shows priests making sacrifices in this way.

## Religious ball game

Mayan and Aztec cities had courts in which people could play a fast-moving ball game. This was believed to represent the battle between life and death, and some experts believe that some of the players were put to death at the end of the game.

INTERNET LINKS

For links to websites where you can learn more about the ancient religions of the Americas, and explore the beliefs of the Maya, Inca and Aztec peoples, go to **www.usborne-quicklinks.com**

115

# RELIGION IN SOCIETY

Religion has been a powerful force in the development of different cultures. In many places religion still has a major influence. Some people feel that religion has had a bad rather than a good influence, causing wars for instance. Others argue that it is not the ideas themselves that have had a bad effect but the way in which they have been misinterpreted and misused. Sometimes, problems which appear to be religious are really just as much to do with racism and politics.

During the late nineteenth century, Mohandas Gandhi dedicated his life to trying to improve society in India. Following the Hindu rule of non-violence, he worked peacefully for ideals such as racial equality. His followers later gave him the name Mahatma, which means "great soul".

*Man becomes great exactly in the degree in which he works for the welfare of his fellow-men.*

*Non-violence is the greatest force at the disposal of mankind. It is mightier than the mightiest weapon of destruction devised by the ingenuity of man.*
Mahatma Gandhi

# Religion and the state

In the past, religion often affected the way in which societies were organized. This meant that people who were thought to be spiritually more important were given greater power. In Europe, kings and queens often claimed to rule by "divine right". This means that they were believed to be God's representatives on Earth. In Japan, emperors claimed to be related to the goddess Amaterasu, and the practice of emperor worship lasted until 1946.

Some countries are still governed by religious leaders. An example is Iran, whose president and government are under the authority of an Islamic religious figure called the Supreme Ruler. Many countries have an official, state religion. This often affects aspects of life such as the law and education.

## Power

Just like any other leaders, religious leaders have sometimes abused their power. If leaders claim to be God's representatives, people may be too frightened to challenge them. People have sometimes been scared into obedience by talk of what will happen to them after death.

During the Middle Ages, for example, some Roman Catholic priests abused their power by promising people a place in heaven after death, in return for money. They also suggested that those who did not obey or pay for forgiveness would burn forever in the fires of hell. In Christianity and Islam, evil has often been represented in the form of the devil, or Satan, who can harm people and tempt them away from God.

Religious charities teach people new skills, so that those they are helping are better able to survive. These Cambodian villagers and charity workers are building a well.

## Caring for others

Although religious power has sometimes been used badly, many people have been inspired by religions to try to change things for the better. Many organized charities have religious origins, for example, Christian Aid and Muslim Aid. Religious charities are often allowed to work in areas that are forbidden to other organizations, for example, war zones.

A lot of charity work has been carried out by religious people who feel that they have a duty to help those who are in trouble. Muslims, for example, believe that giving to charity is a form of worship. Everyone who can has to give a certain percentage of their money to the poor each year.

## INTERNET LINKS

For links to websites about religion in society and where you can find out more about the life of Gandhi and the work of religious charities, go to **www.usborne-quicklinks.com**

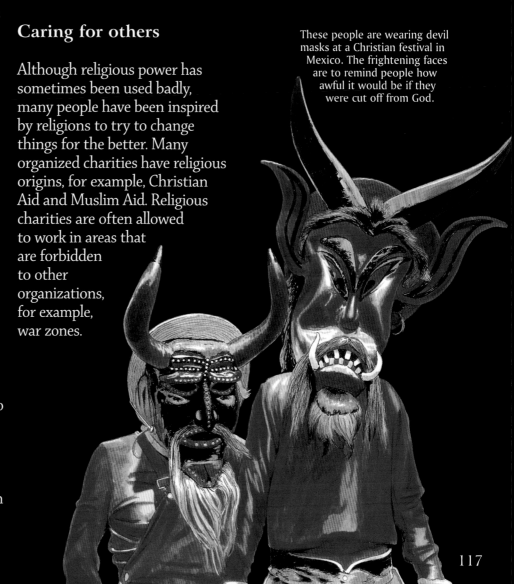

These people are wearing devil masks at a Christian festival in Mexico. The frightening faces are to remind people how awful it would be if they were cut off from God.

## The spread of religions

Some religions feel that they have a duty to try to convert others to their beliefs, either by preaching or by example. This explains in part why some religions have grown so rapidly. Islam spread so quickly after it was first founded at the start of the seventh century that the next six centuries became known as the Golden Age of Islam.

European Christian missionaries (people dedicated to converting others) started working extensively in South and Central America in the sixteenth century, and in Africa and Asia in the eighteenth century. They worked as teachers and in health care, but their main purpose was to convert people from their existing beliefs to Christianity.

In recent years, some people in the Western world have become interested in Eastern religions such as Buddhism and Hinduism. These religions have been brought to the West by people who have visited the East and by people of those faiths who have emigrated to the West.

## Religious war

Rulers have often encouraged their people to go to war by appealing to their religious beliefs. The rulers' motives, however, may sometimes have included their desire for greater political power.

Between about 1095 and 1290CE, for example, armies of European Christians went on a series of armed pilgrimages. These began in response to a speech made by the head of the Catholic Church.

The goal of the Christian armies was to capture Palestine (now Israel). Palestine was ruled by Muslim Turks, and contained a number of important Muslim holy sites. It was also known to to Christians as the Holy Land as Jesus Christ was born there. These armed pilgrimages were called crusades, or holy wars, but they were brutal, and were about power as much as they were about religion.

During the religious wars known as the Crusades, Christian armies fought Muslim Turks for their Holy City, Jerusalem. This fourteenth-century painting shows the Christian knights in Jerusalem.

## Pacifism

Pacifism is the belief that disputes should always be resolved without any violence. Some religions teach that war can never be justified and that believers should never take up arms for any cause. The Jain religion, several Hindu and Buddhist groups and some Christian-related movements such as Quakers and Jehovah's Witnesses are well known for their pacifist beliefs.

Marriage is extremely important in the Unification Church. Members take part in mass weddings, like the one above which took place in Seoul, South Korea, in 1999. Marriage partners are suggested by the Church's leader, Sun Myung Moon.

## Persecution

Where followers of a religion exist in fairly small numbers and do not have much power, they sometimes suffer persecution. Other groups of people may ridicule their beliefs, without understanding them, and try to blame them for things that go wrong in society. This attitude is often accepted by rulers because it moves criticism away from their own failings. Religious prejudice is often combined with racism.

During the 1930s and 1940s, many Jews in Europe were persecuted and forced to wear a star of David to identify them.

When the Jewish people lived scattered in different parts of Europe in the Middle Ages, they became targets for prejudice. Their persecution reached a peak with the Holocaust of World War II (see page 27).

## Separatism

Most religions have some areas of life which they prefer to keep separate from other people. For example, most religions prefer their followers to marry someone of the same religion. Some religious groups, though, prefer to live apart from others as much as they possibly can in order to keep their traditions intact. This may be because of certain rules for living laid down in their scriptures, or it may come about because they feel threatened by persecution.

The Amish, for example, are a group of Christians in North America. They live simple lives in line with their interpretation of the scriptures. They also have strict rules, and live in communities separated from the rest of society. They will not take part in government and reject modern technologies as evil.

## New religious movements

New religious movements are sometimes called sects or cults. Strictly speaking, a sect is a group which breaks away from an established religion. A cult is a group which follows particular rituals of worship.

All the major religions started off as sects or cults, but both words have come to be used in a negative way. This is because many people feel that some, though not all, new religious movements may harm their members.

Some psychologists think that these types of groups appeal to people who are very unhappy and feel themselves to be outsiders. These people may think that a sect or cult gives them a sense of purpose and a feeling of belonging to a group. Sometimes they may become so attached to the group that they will do anything the leader tells them to. This can include breaking off all contact with their family and friends.

The Unification Church is a new religious movement. Its members are nicknamed Moonies after their leader, Sun Myung Moon.

INTERNET LINKS

For links to websites about religion in society, the Amish, and the spread of major religions, go to **www.usborne-quicklinks.com**

## Architecture

Nearly every religion has a special building where worship takes place. Great care is often taken to make this building beautiful so that it is felt to be worthy of the faith, and will encourage praise and spiritual thought. Communities often give money to pay for the materials and may physically help construct the building, which becomes a focal point of the town or village.

In the past, the wealth and engineering skill which went into building places of worship were quite stunning. The engineering was particularly impressive because the builders had far less technology to help them than there is today.

Christians have often designed ornate churches to give glory to God. The craftsmen who carved these spires on the Votive Church in Vienna, Austria, paid painstaking attention to detail, even though the carvings are so high up that people on the ground can't see them clearly.

## Education

Almost all religions emphasize the need for education and see it as their duty to encourage learning. In the past, many people were taught to read and write so they could study religious scriptures.

Sometimes, however, religious authorities try to suppress knowledge that they think might weaken religious belief. In the seventeenth century, for example, the Italian scientist Galileo supported the discovery that the Earth moves around the Sun, not vice versa. The Christian authorities in Italy made him publicly deny this claim or face torture.

In the 1600s, the Christian Church feared that people would lose their faith if they knew that the Earth was not the middle of the universe, as they believed the *Bible* said.

Sun

Earth

## Women

Historically, many religions have not given women equal status with men and have not allowed them to take part in some aspects of religious life. This is generally because women didn't have equal status in the societies where the religions first developed.

Conservative branches of some religions often resist change because they believe that certain traditions were laid down by God. In recent years, however, some religious organizations have changed their rules to allow women to play a greater role in their official structure. For example, Progressive Jewish groups now allow women to lead worship.

## Religious art

Many religious ideas are difficult to express in words. People have always tried to express these ideas, along with the feelings that they inspire, in works of art.

Works of art have always been, and still continue to be, created in order to inspire religious faith. Before people were educated enough to be able to read, paintings and sculptures were a way of teaching a religion's most important beliefs.

Some religious art is considered sacred. For example, statues (called *murtis*) of Hindu gods are thought to contain the presence of the god or goddess whom they represent.

Many Christian stories were elaborately illustrated by monks. This eleventh-century illuminated manuscript shows scenes from the story of the birth of Jesus.

## ┌INTERNET LINKS┐

For links to websites where you can discover more about religion in society and see fabulous examples of religious artwork and architecture, go to **www.usborne-quicklinks.com**

## Music and dancing

Many religions teach that the most effective kind of worship is that which involves a person's body as well as their soul. This has led to religious music being composed and performed, and the development of special religious dances.

This Balinese dancer is performing the *Ramayana*, an ancient Hindu dance. Hindu dances tell stories about the gods through gestures, known as *mudras*. Each of these expresses a particular idea.

Music helps to create an atmosphere in which people can feel and express emotions such as awe and joy, and both music and dance can tell stories. They can also be a way of entering into a trance-like state of meditation through the repetition of rhythmic sounds or movements.

Some religious groups disapprove of music and dancing. This is because such physical pleasures are thought to distract people from the more spiritual aspects of life.

121

# MAP OF RELIGIONS

This map shows the main religions in different parts of the world. The main religion is the one which has a clear majority of an area's population claiming to be followers (see page 5 for an explanation of how religious believers are counted). It is not necessarily the official state religion.

Stripes indicate that there are two or more main religions in an area, each with roughly equal numbers of followers. For instance, in Mongolia the population is divided between Mahayana Buddhism, local religions and state atheism. This is shown by gold, dark pink and lilac stripes.

In addition to the religions shown in a country, there may be many others that are followed there. For example, although the majority of people in India are Hindu, there are several other religions there too. Also, the influence of local religions is often greater than it appears from statistics, especially in Africa and South America.

## Key to the map of world religions

Christianity

Catholic

Protestant

Orthodox

Islam

Sunni

Shi'ah

Buddhism

Mahayana

Theravada

Hinduism

Judaism

Sikhism

Shinto

Confucianism

Local religions

State atheism

NORTH AMERICA

SOUTH AMERICA

This map is not drawn to scale.

Religions are not confined to areas where they are shown on the map. For example, Israel is the only country with Judaism as its main religion, yet only about a quarter of the world's Jews live in Israel. Nearly half of them live in the USA and the rest are scattered throughout the world.

The numbers of people living in different parts of the world vary enormously, so large expanses of one religion on this map do not necessarily mean large numbers of followers. Areas of low population include those on the northern edges of the map, northern and central Australia and the Sahara desert in north Africa.

INTERNET LINKS

For links to websites where you can print out country maps and find charts and information about religions around the world, go to **www.usborne-quicklinks.com**

EUROPE

ASIA

AFRICA

AUSTRALIA

# TIME CHART

This time chart will help you see at a glance when most of the major religions in the world first began. Many of the starting dates are approximate, and faded lines to the left of the chart indicate that nobody really knows quite how far back the religion goes. The right-hand side of the time chart shows the present day.

Local religions go back much further than the earliest date shown on this chart. Evidence has been found of religious belief dating right back to 35,000BCE.

Religions which have all but died out are shown in purple. Some purple lines, for example those which show the religion of the Celtic people, are faded at the right and reach to the present day. These show that some people still have beliefs based on those faiths.

You can see from the chart that the religions that more-or-less died out are not necessarily very ancient. For example, according to this chart, the Inca and Aztec religions were relatively recent, although they did include many beliefs of earlier peoples.

Across the top of the chart you will find some of the key events in the history of the different religions. The tint of the boxes shows the particular religion for which an event is significant.

c.3500BCE Writing developed in Mesopotamia.

c.3000BCE Egypt becomes a united kingdom.

c.1750BCE Aryans enter Indus Valley.

4000BCE 3500BCE 3000BCE 2500BCE 2000BCE 1500BCE

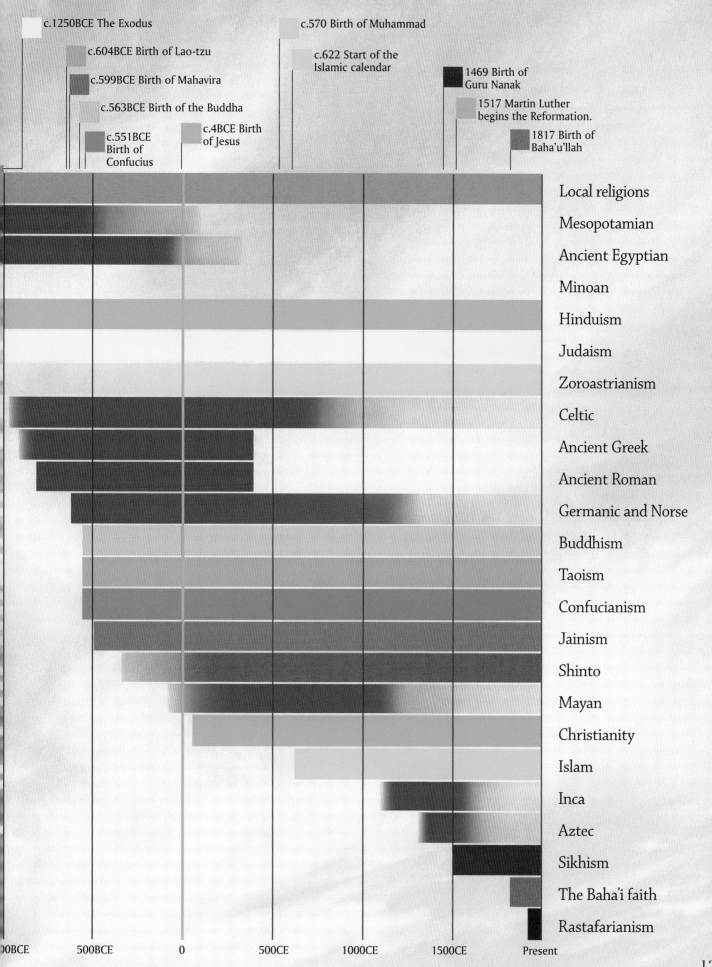

c.1250BCE The Exodus

c.604BCE Birth of Lao-tzu

c.599BCE Birth of Mahavira

c.563BCE Birth of the Buddha

c.551BCE Birth of Confucius

c.4BCE Birth of Jesus

c.570 Birth of Muhammad

c.622 Start of the Islamic calendar

1469 Birth of Guru Nanak

1517 Martin Luther begins the Reformation.

1817 Birth of Baha'u'llah

Local religions

Mesopotamian

Ancient Egyptian

Minoan

Hinduism

Judaism

Zoroastrianism

Celtic

Ancient Greek

Ancient Roman

Germanic and Norse

Buddhism

Taoism

Confucianism

Jainism

Shinto

Mayan

Christianity

Islam

Inca

Aztec

Sikhism

The Baha'i faith

Rastafarianism

| 00BCE | 500BCE | 0 | 500CE | 1000CE | 1500CE | Present |

# INDEX

126

# ACKNOWLEDGEMENTS

Cover designer: Tom Lalonde

Illustrators: Leonard Le Rolland, Verinder Bhachu, Nicholas Hewetson,
Simone Boni, Ian Jackson, Radhi Parekh, Ross Watton

Digital imagery by Joanne Kirkby

Website researchers: Sarah Khan and Jacqueline Clark

Picture researchers: Ruth King and Valerie Modd

American editor: Carrie A Armstrong

Every effort has been made to trace the copyright holders of the material in this book.
If any rights have been omitted, the publishers offer to rectify this in any future edition,
following notification. The publishers are grateful to the following organizations and
individuals for their contribution and permission to reproduce material.

## Photography credits (t = top, m = middle, b = bottom, l = left, r = right)

**Cover** (t) ©Jon Arnold Images Ltd/Alamy, (b) ©Reinhard Dirscherl/Alamy; **p1** ©Lindsay Hebberd/CORBIS; **p2** ©Kevin R Morris/CORBIS; **p5** ©1997 PhotoDisc Inc.; **p6** ©Christine Osborne/CORBIS; **p7** (b) ©Dennis Degnan/CORBIS; **pp8-9** (b) ©1996 PhotoDisc, Inc.; **p9** (t) ©Patrick Ward/CORBIS, (l) ©1996 PhotoDisc Inc.; **p10** ©Stephanie Colasanti/CORBIS; **p11** (tr) ©<CRDPHOTO>/CORBIS, (l) ©Digital Vision; **p12** ©Chloe Johnson; Eye Ubiquitous/CORBIS; **p13** (b) ©Archivo Iconografico, S.A./CORBIS; **pp14-15** ©Bennett Dean; Eye Ubiquitous/CORBIS; **pp16-17** ©Angelo Hornak/CORBIS; **pp18-19** (main) ©Archivo Iconografico, S.A./CORBIS; **p18** ©David Samuel Robbins/CORBIS; **p20** ©David Samuel Robbins/CORBIS; **p21** ©Brian Vikander/CORBIS; **p22** ©Albrecht G. Shaefer/CORBIS; **p23** ©Lindsay Hebberd/CORBIS; **p24** ©Ted Spiegel/CORBIS; **p25** (br) ©Gianni Dagli Orti/CORBIS; **p27** ©Richard T. Nowitz/CORBIS; **pp28-29** ©Richard T. Nowitz/CORBIS; **p29** (tl) ©Ted Spiegel/CORBIS; **p30** (tm) ©ArkReligion.com/H Rogers, (b) ©Barry Lewis/CORBIS; **p31** ©David H. Wells/CORBIS; **p32** (t) ©Ted Spiegel/CORBIS, (bl) ©1997 PhotoDisc, Inc.; **p33** ©Owen Franken/CORBIS; **p34** ©Richard T. Nowitz/CORBIS; **p35** (t) ©Richard T. Nowitz/CORBIS, (br) ©2001 PhotoDisc, Inc.; **p36** ©Alison Wright/CORBIS; **p37** (t), (br) ©1996 Photodisc, Inc.; **pp38-39** ©Alison Wright/CORBIS; **p39** (t) ©1997 Photodisc, Inc.; **p40** (l) ©Craig Lovell/CORBIS; **p41** ©Owen Franken/CORBIS; **pp42-43** (main) ©Abbie Enock; Travel Ink/CORBIS; **p43** (t) ©Chris Lisle/CORBIS; **pp44-45** (main) ©Wolfgang Kaehler/CORBIS; **p45** (tr), (mr) ©1997 Photodisc, Inc.; **p46** ©Earl & Nazima Kowall/CORBIS; **p47** ©David Samuel Robbins/CORBIS; **p48** ©David Lees/CORBIS; **p49** (t) ©Philadelphia Museum of Art/CORBIS; **p50** ©Archivo Iconografico, S.A./CORBIS; **p51** (r) ©Karen Tweedy-Holmes/CORBIS; **pp52-53** ©Dave Bartruff/CORBIS; **p53** (r) ©Jon Rogers; **p54** (tl) Biblioteca Nacional, Madrid, Spain/Photo © AISA/The Bridgeman Art Library; **p55** (br) ©Bettmann/CORBIS; **p56** ©Patrick Ward/CORBIS; **p57** ©joseph@visionsofamerica.com; **p58** (l) ©Patrick Ward/CORBIS; **p59** ©Angelo Hornak/CORBIS; **p60** ©Morton Beebe, S.F./CORBIS; **p61** (t) ©2001 PhotoDisc Inc; (m), (bl) ©Jon Rogers; **p62** (t) ©Owen Franken/CORBIS, (bl) ©1996 Photodisc, Inc., (br) ©Jon Rogers; **p63** (main) ©Charles & Josette Lenars/CORBIS, (r) ©1996 Photodisc, Inc.; **p64** (tr) ©Paul Almasy/CORBIS; (l) ©David Cumming; Eye Ubiquitous/CORBIS; **p65** ©Richard Hamilton Smith/CORBIS; **p66** ©Richard Cummins/CORBIS; **p67** ©Nick Wiseman; Eye Ubiquitous/CORBIS; **p68** ©Chris Lisle/CORBIS; **p69** (t) ©Michael Holford; **p70** (m) ©Jon Rogers, (b) ©ArkReligion.com/ H Rogers; **p71** ©Nik Wheeler/CORBIS; **pp72-73** ©Richard T. Nowitz/CORBIS; **p74** ©ArkReligion.com/H Rogers; **p75** (l) ©2001 PhotoDisc, Inc., (r) ©Charles and Josette Lenars/CORBIS, (b) ©Jon Rogers; **p76** ©The Purcell Team/CORBIS; **p77** ©Sheldan Collins/CORBIS; **p78** ©Francoise de Mulder/CORBIS; **p79** ©Annie Griffiths Belt/CORBIS; **p80** ©Michael Freeman/CORBIS; **p81** (b) ©ArkReligion.com/H Rogers; **p82** ©ArkReligion.com/H Rogers; **p83** ©Gunter Marx/CORBIS; **pp84-85** ©Bennett Dean; Eye Ubiquitous/CORBIS; **p86** ©Chris Lisle/CORBIS; **p87** ©Eye Ubiquitous/Hutchison; **p88** (t) ©Earl & Nazima Kowall/CORBIS; **pp88-89** ©Chris Lisle/CORBIS; **pp90-91** ©Michael Freeman/CORBIS; **p92** ©Neil Beer/CORBIS; **p93** (t) ©Nathan Benn/CORBIS; **p94** ©Werner Forman Archive; **p95** ©Chris Lisle/CORBIS; **p97** (tr) ©1996 PhotoDisc, Inc., (b) ©ArkReligion.com/P Kerry; **p98** ©Brian Vikander/CORBIS; **p99** ©Daniel Lainé/CORBIS; **p100** ©Studio Patellani/CORBIS; **p101** ©Lindsay Hebberd/CORBIS; **p102** (t) ©Penny Tweedie/CORBIS, (b) ©Paul A. Souders/CORBIS; **p103** ©Paul A. Souders/CORBIS; **p104** ©Layne Kennedy/CORBIS; **p105** ©ArkReligion.com/A Kuznetsov; **p106** (m) ©Morton Beebe, S.F./CORBIS; **pp106-107** ©Peter Reynolds; Frank Lane Picture Agency/CORBIS; **p107** ©David Lees/CORBIS; **p108** (b) ©Michael Nicholson/CORBIS; **pp108-109** ©Michael Holford; **p110** (t) ©Christel Gerstenberg/CORBIS; **p111** ©Charles O'Rear/CORBIS; **pp112-113** ©Michael Nicholson/CORBIS; **p113** ©Adam Woolfitt/CORBIS; **p114** ©Nevada Wier/CORBIS; **p115** (t) ©Michael Holford, (b) ©1996 PhotoDisc, Inc.; **p116** ©Bettmann/CORBIS; **p117** (t) ©Howard Davies/CORBIS; **pp118-119** ©Photo Scala, Florence; **p119** (t) ©Reuters Newmedia Inc./CORBIS; **p120** (l) ©Danita Delimont/Alamy; (r) ©Digital Vision; **p121** (r) ©Dave Bartruff/CORBIS, (l) ©Sandro Vannini/CORBIS; **pp124-125** (background) ©Digital Vision.

This revised edition first published in 2015 by Usborne Publishing Ltd,
Usborne House, 83-85 Saffron Hill, London EC1N 8RT, England. www.usborne.com